Study Guide to Accompany

Baron and Byrne's

SOCIAL PSYCHOLOGY
Understanding Human Interaction

FOURTH EDITION

Prepared by

Gene F. Smith

Bem P. Allen

Western Illinois University

ALLYN AND BACON, INC.

Boston/London/Sydney/Toronto

CONTENTS

HOW TO USE YOUR STUDY GUIDE

We believe that your instructor has chosen the best possible avenue to learning all about SOCIAL PSYCHOLOGY, the Baron and Byrne text. Baron and Byrne's book is the most comprehensive, up-to-date, interesting account of social psychology that is available. If you master the Baron and Byrne book, you will have a useful grasp of social behavior that will benefit you for years to come.

We also believe that this Study Guide will almost certainly guarantee your mastery of the Baron-Byrne text. Not so incidentally, your Study Guide is such a detailed and systematic approach to the text that careful completion of the exercises in the Guide will almost certainly guarantee you a high grade in your social psychology course.

The first step in mastering a chapter of the text is to read over the objectives for that chapter. Objectives for each chapter are found at the beginning of the Guide chapter that bears the same number as the text chapter you wish to master. The next step is to read the chapter in the text. Look over the objectives and do the reading as soon as the chapter is assigned. Read the chapter before going back to the objectives or you may want to consider the objectives as you read.

After familiarizing yourself with text coverage of objectives for a chapter, do the Guide exercises for that chapter. The first exercise that you will encounter in each Guide chapter is "Who Done It?". The "Who Done It?" items are designed to help you master those objectives that refer to the contributions of notable social psychologists to the understanding of social behavior. Exercise Two is called "Define." The Definition section allows mastery of objectives referring to critical concepts. The next exercise is called "Matching." The "Matching" items will allow you to master objectives which refer to simple concepts. For each matching item, all you have to do is fill in the blank with the letter designating the corresponding item.

Next, do the "Is Something Wrong Here?" exercise. Items for this exercise will help you master objectives that refer to critical statements in the text. Be careful! Each item is either a correct statement from the text or a statement that has been "doctored" so that it looks correct, but has been changed from its original form in the text. The fifth exercise in each Guide chapter is "True-False." This tried and true format (pun intended) will allow you to master objectives that refer to straightforward social psychological principles outlined in the text. The last exercise is "Fill-in-the-Blanks." Also a familiar format, the "Fill-in-the-Blanks" exercise will allow you to master objectives that refer to more difficult concepts covered in the text.

In the six exercises, there is at least one item that corresponds to each objective. Answers are conveniently located near a given exercise. You can immediately find out how you did on the items for an exercise without having to search through answers all crammed together at the end of the chapter. To help you further, the Study Guide includes text page numbers after the answers to exercise items. Should you not understand an item after seeing its answer, you can look up the corresponding concept in the text.

After you have finished the exercises, you will have learned the objectives. In turn, having learned the objectives, you will have mastered the text, because the objectives "zero in" on every important consideration in the text. The night before the test on text chapters, go over objectives recalling how each is covered in the text. Then respond to the multiple choice items near the end of the chapter (correct answers are given just after the items). These items were written by the same people who wrote the test items provided for your instructor (that's us, Smith and Allen). If your test includes these items, you should be especially well prepared. We randomly chose some items for your guide and some for the instructor's test item file, thus guaranteeing that the Guide items are just like the file items. Your instructor has the Guide items also. Perhaps your instructor would be willing to reward your conscientious use of the Guide by including some of the Guide items on the test. If you want to even further assure yourself that you know the material in the text, for a few randomly chosen objectives turn to the text to see if your recollection of how those objectives are covered in the text is accurate. This last task should give you considerable confidence.

Learning the objectives means that you have mastered the text and that you are ready to "ace" the test. And "ace it" is not too strong a statement. Here's why: each multiple-choice item that tests your knowledge of text material has been directly drawn from an objective. If you follow the steps outlined above, you will know the material in the text and you can't help but do well on the test.

Oh, by the way, we have added a section to each Guide chapter that is "Just for Fun." It contains readings from the popular literature on social psychology (for example, Psychology Today). Each reading will be easy to find in your university or college library and each will be exciting to read as well.

GFS   BPA

CHAPTER 1

UNDERSTANDING SOCIAL BEHAVIOR: AN INTRODUCTION

Objectives

1. Discuss the validity of the "wisdom of the ages" (i.e. common
    knowledge) as a source of information about social behavior.
    it is a good starting point but may contain incorrect information.

2. Why study social behavior? *To better understand personal behavior &
    interpersonal behavior*

3. What is the text's working definition of social psychology?
    *the scientific field that seeks to comprehend the nature and causes of individual
    behavior in social situations*

4. What are the three categories of causal factors that influence
    social behavior? *1. behavior & characteristics of other persons
    2. social cognition
    3. the broader social context*

5. Contrast the approaches taken in the early social psychology
    texts of McDougall (1909) and Allport (1924).
    *small number of innate tendencies   many different factors influence social behavior
    cause social behavior*

6. Note the contributions made by Sherif and Lewin to social
    psychology in the 1930s. Note the trends of the 1940s and
    1950s. *the study of social norms / expanded scope of inquiry; development
    of cognitive dissonance theory*

7. Beyond the rapid expansion of existing lines of research and
    the development of new lines, what two current trends continue
    to develop? *1. social cognition
    2. concern with practical matters & applied issues*

8. Outline the basic steps that are followed in an experiment.
    *state hypothesis
    determine variables*
    a) Distinguish between the independent variable and the
    perform experiment   dependent variable. → *the behavior being studied   that which is systematically changed*
    collect data
    analyze data   b) Discuss the studies dealing with the effect of pleasant
    state results   scents on liking.

9. Citing examples, describe the importance of: *scent experiment — if one group all
    had colds*
    a) Random assignment of subjects to groups.
    b) Avoiding confounding of variables. *— scent & dress allowed to
    vary.*

10. What are the advantages and disadvantages of doing experiments *(see pg 21
    Table 1.1)*
    in the laboratory vs. the field? *advantages
    1. more control over variables
    disadvantages   2. less time consuming
    1. less direct relevance of findings   3. less confounding variables
    2. artificiality   4. rights & safety of subjects
    3. more chance of demand characteristics   are more easily protected
    4. restricted subject population.*

1

11. Why is experimentation the most powerful method of social psychological research? *because it is able to determine a cause & effect relationship*

12. What two reasons often make it impossible to use the experimental approach? *1. practical reasons 2. ethical considerations*

13. Focusing on the text's examples, outline the procedure that is followed in a correlational study. *identify variables, determine setting that variables can be observed in, observe behavior, evaluate correlation between the variables*

14. Contrast the experimental and correlational approaches, especially focusing on the advantages of each. *exp. is more powerful; cor. - is more practical*

15. Describe the major disadvantage of the correlational approach, i.e. the causation problem. *it isn't possible to arrive at a cause/effect relationship only to measure the correlation between variables*

16. Describe the role of theory in social psychological research. *Theory is the attempt to answer "why?" to observed behavior.*

17. Why do social psychological researchers often use deception methodology? *To limit the effects from demand characteristics*

18. List potential problems that exist when an investigator uses deception. *1. resentment from subjects 2. possible harm to subjects → after experiment tell subjects of results*

19. Describe the informed concent, debriefing, and confidentiality safeguards. *describe procedures (and risks) as much as possible → protect the rights of subjects by keeping individual response confidential*

20. Why was funding for social psychology research cut so heavily in the spring of 1981? *because it wasn't perceived as having any practical purpose -*

Who Done It?

This section will occur in the other 14 chapters of the Study Guide. Critical studies and important ideas that you should be able to associate with names will be presented. However, Chapter 1 of the text is somewhat different from the remaining chapters, in that it presents few studies. Thus there is no Who Done It? exercise for Chapter 1.

Define

Each of the critical concepts listed below have been defined in your textbook. For each provide the definition. Answers are on the next page.

1. "common knowledge" *information which has been obtained from a variety of sources but which hasn't necessarily been subjected to scientific verification*

2. social psychology *the field of science devoted to understanding how the behavior of others affect the behavior of the individual*

3. the experimental method *the scientific method that used systematic control & measurement of independent variables to understand a particular dependent variable being studied*

4. independent variable *that which is systematically varied in an experiment*

5. dependent variable *that which is being studied*

6. correlational method *the scientific method where observation of 2 or more variables are studied to see how they are related*

7. deception methodology *the use of deception in social/psychology research to protect against demand characteristics*

8. demand characteristics *bias which results from ones idea about what is being studied*

Matching

Match each concept or idea on the left with an identifying phrase, word or sentence on the right. Answers are at the bottom of the page. Cover them until you've completed the exercise.

A. opposite of confounding   D 1. studied by Sherif in 1930s
B. common knowledge   E 2. uninformed experimenter
C. correlational studies   A 3. hold extraneous variables constant
D. social norms   F 4. role of theory
E. reduces demand character-   B 5. "wisdom of the ages"
    istics   G 6. experimental safeguard
F. explanation   H 7. studied by Lewin in 1930s
G. confidentiality   C 8. ambiguous regarding cause-
H. leadership and other group   and-effect
    processes

Matching Answers

1. D (13)   5. B (4)
2. E (20)   6. G (28)
3. A (18)   7. H (13)
4. F (25)   8. C (23)

3

Definitions

1. the informal information that has accumulated in a variety of ways, but that has never been tested by scientific methods (4)

2. the scientific field that studies how the behavior, feelings, and/or thoughts of a person are affected by other persons (6)

3. research approach in which one factor is systematically varied to test its effects upon the subject's behavior (15-16)

4. the factor that is systematically varied in an experiment (16)

5. the aspect of the subject's behavior that is measured by the experimenter to determine if it is affected by the independent variable (16)

6. research approach in which two variables are measured to determine whether changes in one variable are associated with changes in the second (22)

7. research procedure used in experiments; involves withholding information from the subjects or deliberately providing false information in some cases (27)

8. any aspect of the experimental situation which allows the subject to determine the hypothesis of the study (20)

Is Something Wrong Here?

For each statement below indicate what is wrong about the statement, if anything. If there _is_ something wrong, answer "yes" and indicate what's wrong. If nothing is wrong, answer "No; this one is correct." At the end of this exercise you will find the answers.

yes 1. Common knowledge is ~~totally useless as a~~ source of information about social behavior. _a good place to begin seeking_

yes 2. According to the text's working definition, social psychology is a ~~non~~scientific field.

yes 3. The first _Social Psychology_ text by McDougall in 1908 was ~~amazingly close to~~ current social psychology in that it ~~con~~tained reports of actual research on several topics. _far removed, did not, from_

_no_ 4. _this one is correct_ Your text argues that two trends that developed in social psychology in the 1970s and have expanded in the 1980s were greater concern with applied issues and the development of the social cognition perspective.

yes 5. In experimental studies of the effect of wearing a pleasant scent, the independent variable has typically ~~been some index~~ of ~~the person's likability.~~ _the scent worn_

4

yes 6. There has been ~~a decrease~~ *an increase* in the use of correlational methods in social psychology in the past few years.

yes 7. Most theories in social psychology *do not* consist of mathematical equations, *rather of verbal statements*

yes 8. If the predictions derived from a theory are not supported by research findings, the only option is *not* to reject the theory, *but to vary the research*

yes 9. In deception experiments, the term confederate ~~simply~~ refers to the person ~~who is the subject in the experiment.~~ *is used to deceive the subject in some way.*

yes 10. The major reason social psychologists employ deception methodology is ~~that they enjoy watching people fall for the false information.~~ *to limit the effects of demand characteristics*

no, this is correct 11. Most social psychologists believe that it is permissible to use deception if it is accompanied by informed consent and thorough debriefing.

Is Something Wrong Here? Answers

1. Yes; common knowledge is often contradictory and sometimes wrong, but it does contain insights that can be investigated by social psychologists. (4)

2. Yes; social psychology is, of course, a scientific field. (6)

3. Yes; it was not until the 1924 text of Allport that reports of actual research were included. (12)

4. No; this one is correct. (14)

5. Yes; the independent variable is the presence of the scent, the dependent variable is the measure of liking. (17)

6. Yes; actually, there has been a small increase due to the development of techniques for determining cause and effect from correlational data. (24)

7. Yes; most consist of verbal statements, including definitions of basic concepts and statements concerning the relationship between these concepts. (25)

8. Yes; theories need not be rejected, they are always subject to modification. (26)

9. Yes; a confederate is an employee of the experimenter who pretends to be a subject, thereby deceiving the real subject. (27)

10. Wrong, of course; the major reason is that if subjects knew what was being studied, their behavior would often be affected by their knowledge. (27)

11. No; this one is correct.(28)

True-False

Indicate whether each of the following statements is true or false. Correct answers are at the end of this exercise.

 1. The characteristic which distinguishes science from nonscience is the topic which is studied. *F*

 2. The results of laboratory studies have greater generalizability than studies conducted in the field. *F*

 3. Demand characteristics are more often present in laboratory settings than in field settings. *T*

 4. Practical limitations and ethical restrictions are the two factors that often make the use of the experimental approach impossible. *T*

 5. The preferred method of research by social psychologists has generally been the experimental method. *T*

 6. If two variables are correlated with each other, it is certain that one of them is a cause and the other an effect. *F*

 7. Experimental methods are always preferred over correlational methods. *F*

 8. Social psychologists use deception methodology more than researchers in other fields. *T*

 9. Most subjects who learn that they've been deceived in an experiment resent having been fooled. *F*

10. Social psychology has been of practical benefit and has been duly recognized for its contributions. *F*

True-False Answers

 1. False; the use of scientific <u>methods</u> and <u>techniques</u> is the distinguishing feature.(7)

 2. False; field studies have greater generalizability because of the more diverse sample of subjects generally attracted.(20)

3. True (20)

4. True (21)

5. True (22)

6. False; it is possible that a third variable is causing the variation in both variables. (23)

7. False; while experimental methods are generally preferred, correlational techniques often make a valuable contribution.
(23)

8. True (27)

9. False; in fact, most subjects seem to react quite positively. (29)

10. False; the text asserts that social psychology has been of great practical benefit, but has <u>not</u> been given credit for its contributions. (30)

Fill-in-the-Blanks

Complete the following statements by filling in the blanks with correct information. The answers are at the end of this exercise.

1. The approximate year in which social psychology emerged as an independent field of study was _1908—1924_.

2. The important theory which suggests that people are motivated to eliminate inconsistency between attitudes or between attitudes and behavior is _cognitive dissonance theory_.

3. The factor which is systematically varied by an experimenter is the _independent_ variable.

4. Behavior that is performed by the subject and measured by the experimenter is the basis for the _dependent_ variable.

5. The method of investigation being employed when an investigator systematically varies the independent variable in order to determine its impact on the dependent variable is the _experimental_ method.

7

6. When an investigator includes more than one independent variable in an experiment to determine whether the impact of one independent variable is affected by the value of the others, the investigator is testing for _interaction_.

7. According to the principle of _random assignment_, each person participating in an experiment must have an equal chance of being exposed to each level of the independent variable.

8. When it is impossible to determine whether the results of a study are due to the independent variable or some other factor that varied simultaneously with the independent variable, this is called _confounding_ of variables.

9. In order to avoid the two potential pitfalls of experimentation, experiments should _randomize_ and avoid _confounding_ of variables.

10. Cues in an experimental setting which serve to communicate the hypothesis of the study to the subjects are called _demand characteristics_.

11. The research method which is best able to establish a cause-and-effect relationship is the _experimental_ method.

12. When careful, systematic observation is made of two naturally-occurring variables to determine whether there is a relationship between them the _correlational_ method is being used.

13. The most important source of research ideas in the field of social psychology is _theory_.

14. Testable propositions, often derived from theories, are called _hypothesis_.

15. The procedure in which subjects are provided with information about any upsetting, frightening, or threatening aspects of an experiment prior to their participation so that they can withdraw if they wish is called *informed consent*.

16. The full description provided to the subject after he has completed his participation in an experiment is called ___*debriefing*___.

17. The reason that data gathered from subjects should be coded, so that it cannot be identified with participants' names is to help maintain strict *confidentiality*.

Fill-in-the-Blanks Answers

1. somewhere between 1908 and 1924 (12)
2. cognitive dissonance theory (13)
3. independent (16)
4. dependent (16)
5. experimental (16)
6. interaction (17)
7. random assignment (17)
8. confounding (18)
9. randomly assign subjects to groups; confounding (18)
10. demand characteristics (20)
11. experimental (19)
12. correlational (22)
13. theory (24)
14. hypotheses (26)
15. informed consent (28)
16. debriefing (28)
17. confidentiality (28)

1. Your text's evaluation of the "wisdom of the ages" as a source
    of information regarding social behavior is that
    a. it does not contain even a kernel of truth
    b. it has conclusively answered most questions of interest to
        social psychologists
    c. it has been raised to its current status by the findings of
        social psychologists
    d. there are enough contradictions in its statements to make
        it an unreliable source of information
    e. both b and c

    d

2. Social psychology is the study of
    a. how people should behave
    b. how people's behavior is affected by social situations
    c. the relationship between common knowledge and actual be-
        havior
    d. social institutions, such as schools, churches, and govern-
        ments

    b

3. According to the text, social psychology emerged as an indepen-
    dent field of study
    a. somewhere between 1908 and 1924
    b. after 1945
    c. in the 1960s
    d. in the 1970s

    a

4. Which statement best characterizes present-day social psych-
    ology?
    a. It is a mature field, with standard topics of research that
        have changed little in the past decade.
    b. Research activity has declined in the past decade.
    c. Social psychologists have quit doing experiments and are
        now doing mainly correlational studies.
    d. It is a growing and rapidly changing field.

    d

5. An experimenter varies the temperature level in order to
    determine its effect on aggression. The level of aggression
    shown by the subject is the _____ variable.
    a. independent
    b. dependent
    c. intervening
    d. correlated

    b

6. A researcher conducts a study in which subjects interact with a
    stranger (an accomplice of the researcher). This person wears
    either perfume, garlic juice, or pine-scented arosol. After
    interacting with the stranger, subjects indicate their liking
    for her. What is the <u>independent</u> variable in this study?
    a. the physical appearance of the accomplice
    b. subjects' ratings of their liking or disliking for her
    c. the substance worn by the accomplice
    d. there is none; this study is based solely on informal
        observation

    c

10

7. A researcher wishes to study the impact of speed of speech on persuasion. To do so, she varies the speed with which an accomplice delivers a prepared speech, so that it is either slow, moderate, or fast. Inadvertently, the accomplice also adds more expression to his voice when delivering the fast speech than when delivering the slow one. This is an example of:
    a. an interaction between two variables
    b. the confounding of two variables
    c. good experimental design
    d. the random assignment of subjects to groups

b

8. The opposite of confounding between variables is to
    a. find statistically significant results
    b. do a correlational study
    c. vary several factors simultaneously
    d. hold constant all other factors while varying the independent variable

d

9. The text mentions the possibility of keeping the person collecting the data in an experiment "in the dark" about the hypothesis of the study. What's the reason for this?
    a. it increases the likelihood of finding differences between the conditions
    b. it reduces the need to use deception
    c. it reduces the possibility of unethical behavior by the experimenter
    d. it reduces the likelihood of demand characteristics

d

10. _____ limitations prevent us from using experimental methods to study the effect that height has on the success of political candidates.
    a. practical   c. ethical
    b. observational   d. correlational

a

11. Which is an advantage of the correlational method?
    a. it is especially well adapted to laboratory research
    b. it is powerful with regard to demonstrating cause-and-effect relationships
    c. it can be used to study questions which for practical or ethical reasons, cannot be studied experimentally
    d. all of the above

c

12. If we observe the amount of aggression occurring on particular days and also record the temperature on those days to determine whether aggression and temperature are related, we are using the _____ method
    a. experimental
    b. correlational
    c. case study
    d. not enough information is provided to allow a choice between a and b

b

11

13. Assume that a carefully done correlational study has found that *d*
    the more crowded the living conditions in a given area, the
    higher the crime rate. On the basis of this study one could
    conclude that
    a. crowding causes crime
    b. being a criminal causes the person to seek a crowded place
       to live
    c. the poorer people are, the smaller the living quarters they
       can afford and also the more likely they are to engage in
       crime
    d. a correlational study does not allow one to choose from
       among the above interpretations

14. The goal of theory is to _____ various aspects of social *a*
    behavior
    a. explain   d. control
    b. observe   e. predict
    c. describe

Just for Fun: Some Additional Readings

Broad, W.J. and Wade, N. Science's faulty fraud detectors. Psychology Today, November, 1982, pp. 51ff. More vigilance is needed
   so that the "system" is not abused; scientists need to repeat one
   another's experiments, for example.

Rubin, Zick. Jokers Wild in the Lab. Psychology Today, December,
   1970, pp. 81 ff. A brief introduction to the use of deception
   in social psychological research, possible ethical implications,
   and possible alternative methods.

Warwick, Donald P. Social scientists ought to stop lying. Psychology
   Today, February, 1975, pp. 38 ff. A sociologist argues that
   social scientists should quit using deception.

Rosenthal, Robert. Self-fulfilling prophecy. Psychology Today,
   Septmeber, 1968. The effects of people's expectations on
   various types of behavior is explored. One type of expectation
   that may influence behavior, it is pointed out, is the expectation of a psychological experimenter.

CHAPTER 2

SOCIAL PERCEPTION:

KNOWING OTHERS...AND OURSELVES

Objectives

1. What is the single most important source of information regard-
    ing the feelings of others? Why is it that this source often
    fails? *verbal communication* / *because others refrain from providing
    the information*

2. What are the six emotions represented by their own distinct
    facial expressions? Are, we capable of showing only six
    different emotions? *happiness, sadness, surprise, fear, anger, disgust
    no, there are many combinations of the six types*

3. Cite evidence supporting the idea that humans <u>show</u> universal
    facial expressions and that they universally <u>recognize</u> the
    meaning of such facial expressions. *studies done in New Guinea by Ekman
    & Friesen.*

4. Describe how display rules limit the universal occurrence of
    facial expressions. *by causing cultural rules and learning to override
    the universal tendencies*

5. At what age do infants show discrete facial expressions closely *1-2 months*
    related to their emotional states? What role do these expres-
    sions play in social development? *they transmit important information to caregivers
    form strong affective bond between infant & parent*

6. Describe the facial feedback hypothesis, indicating how sup- *→ classical
    pressed or exaggerated facial expressions affect what we feel.* *conditioning*
    the view that facial expressions can strongly affect our emotional state

7. What is communicated by a high level of eye contact? by a low
    level of eye contact? *sign of liking (positive feelings)* *unfriendliness
    avoidance*

8. What kind of negative feelings and behavioral reactions occur
    when another person stares, at us? Note also how stares affect
    helping. *anger & hostility*

9. What body language cues suggest emotional arousal? What do
    emblems communicate? What body language cues suggest liking
    and disliking? *→ cultural specific information*
    large amount of movement *facing someone else,
    leaning in their direction,
    nodding agreement*
    *avoiding facing others
    leaning away
    looking at the ceiling
    shaking heads in disagreement*

15

10. What behaviors are related to individual differences in expressiveness? *body language ; non-verbal cues*

11. Describe the relationship between femininity/masculinity and expressiveness. Why do traditional females differ from traditional males in expressiveness? *because of societal norms*

12. Summarize the findings of Sabatelli, Buck, and Dryer (1983) regarding the impact of expressiveness on marital adjustment. *better wive's ability to read nonverbal messages from husband — fewer complaints / better husband's ability to send good — fewer complaints*

attempt to develop a mental analysis of the social world

13. Describe the attribution process; what two factors complicate the task of making trait inferences from observed behavior? *others deception of true traits + the effects of external factors*

14. List the five factors that determine whether we form a correspondent inference, according to Jones and Davis (1965). Describe how each factor affects our attribution. *occurred by choice, uncommon effects, social undesirability*

15. Summarize how consensus, consistency, and distinctiveness information affect our decision regarding whether someone's action is internally or externally caused. *others act similarly / person acts similarly to stimulus / the extent to which they act similarly to other stimuli*

16. Under what circumstances are we "cognitive misers"? *when we respond to isolated situations*

17. Describe the underutilization of consensus and why it occurs. *not taking others behavior into account / because we relize that individuals differ greatly*

18. Describe the circumstances under which we use the discounting principle and the augmenting principle. *when we must try to understand a person's behavior on the basis of a single incident*

19. List dimensions other than the familiar internal-external one on which causal attributions vary. *simple — complex ; good — bad. enduring — transient*

20. Describe the fundamental attribution error, indicate why it occurs, and note how it can be reversed. *overestimating the role of disposition / focusing on actions rather than context / by focusing on the situation rather than the person*

21. Describe the actor/observer effect, and indicate how it can be reversed. *attributing our own behavior to external (situational) causes and others to internal ones / by empathizing with others (putting ourselves in their spot)*

if I do so good its from within if I do bad it is situational

22. Describe self-serving bias and the ego-defensive and self-presentational explanations for it. Summarize the conditions under which ego-defensive and self-presentational processes operate. What are the costs and benefits of the self-serving strategy? *ability is viewed more positively, but honesty + modesty suffer.*

23. Consider the practical implications of attributional errors as presented in the "Applied" box.

what we do serves as a guide to what to attribute to myself.

24. Describe the basic idea underlying Bem's theory of self-perception; when is it that we are most likely to use overt actions as a guide to our attitudes and emotions? *We come to know our own attitudes or emotions partly by inferring them from observations of our overt behavior*

25. What happens when a person is offered extra rewards for taking part in intrinsically appealing activities? Under what circumstances does this "overjustification effect" fail to occur? *often appeal is lowered*

1) when initial interest is made salient
2) when rewards are offered as a sign of competence, or effectiveness
3) when rewards are substantial

emotion—provoking events elicit internal arousal, which causes us to look outward to discover the basis for its presence; then we label the emotion

26. Summarize the process by which we come to know our own emotional states, according to Schachter's theory; describe the experiments done to support the theory. *used epinephrine to heighten arousal then presented emotional situations to two groups; one that understood the effects*

27. Describe the attributional therapy used by Wilson and Linville (1982). *inducing individuals to reattribute their problems to external rather than internal causes / stemming mainly from temporary causes* *the drug would produce & one that didn't*

Who Done It?

Credit each of the concepts, theories, critical studies or important ideas listed below to the person or persons associated with each (e.g., item: Id-Ego-Superego; associated person: Freud). Answers are on the next page.

1. originally proposed theory of correspondent inference *Jones & Davis*

2. attribution is based on consensus, distinctiveness, and consistency *Kelley*

3. theory of self-perception *Bem*

4. study on how masculinity/femininity is related to the use of nonverbal cues *Zuckerman*

5. study of effectiveness of "attribution therapy" with college freshmen *Wilson & Linville*

6. study that revealed self-serving bias resulting from feedback about test performance *Greenberg, Pyszczynski, Solmon*

Define

Each of the critical concepts listed below have been defined in your textbook. For each provide the definition. Answers are on the next page.

1. facial feedback hypothesis *the theory that our feeling of emotion is dependent upon facial expressions we use.*

2. attribution — *the process by which we endeavor to understand other people.*

3. personalism — *the more we perceive another's behavior as being meant to harm or help us, the more we ascribe it to stable dispositions*

4. hedonic relevance — *the more personal another's behavior effects us, the more we view it in terms of disposition*

5. the discounting principle *tendency to downgrade individual causes for behavior when more than one cause is evident*

6. the fundamental attribution error — *the tendency to overuse trait attributes to describe others behavior*

7. actor-observer difference in attribution — *tendency to attribute our actions to situation and others to internal traits*

8. self-serving bias *we view our own internal traits as the cause of positive outcomes, and our own failure as due to situational factors*

17

Who Done It? Answers

1. Jones and Davis (56) *correspondent inference*
2. Kelley (57) *attribution based on consensus, constancy, distinctiveness*
3. Bem (71) *theory of self-perception*
4. Zuckerman, et al. (52) *male/female and non verbal cues*
5. Wilson and Linville (76) *attribution therapy with college students*
6. Greenberg, Pysczynski, and Solmon (66) *self-serving bias stems from desire to protect self esteem*

Definition Answers

1. the idea that the emotion we experience is affected by the facial expression that we portray (46) *facial feedback hypothesis*

2. the process by which we seek to understand others; basically, we seek to do this by observing their behavior and drawing conclusions from it (54) *attribution*

3. when we perceive another person's behavior as intended to harm or benefit us, we are more likely to attribute it to stable dispositions (57) *personalism*

4. the greater the impact of another person's behavior upon us, the more we perceive it as stemming from his/her lasting dispositions (56) *hedonic relevance*

5. when more than one potential cause is present for some behavior, we tend to downgrade the perceived importance of each particular cause (60) *the discounting principle*

6. refers to our tendency to overuse trait attributions when describing other peoples' behavior (64) *the fundamental attribution error*

7. we tend to attribute our own behavior to situational factors, and the behavior of others to their traits (64) *actor/observer difference in attribution*

8. our tendency to view our own traits as the cause of our positive outcomes, and situational factors as the cause of our negative outcomes (66) *self serving bias*

18

Matching

Match each concept or idea on the left with an identifying phrase, word or sentence on the right. Answers are at the bottom of this page.

A. moods, feelings, emotions
B. attribution
C. cognitive miser
D. nonverbal cues
E. smile
F. classical conditioning
G. conveys emotional arousal
H. overjustification effect

_D_ 1. often reveal "concealed" feelings
_F_ 2. underlies effect of facial expressions on feelings
_A_ 3. temporary causes
_C_ 4. does as little attributional work as possible
_H_ 5. caused by large extrinsic rewards
_G_ 6. a large amount of body movement
_E_ 7. a universally recognized sign (other than D)
_B_ 8. relatively lasting causes are inferred

Is Something Wrong Here?

For each statement below indicate what is wrong about the statement, if anything. If there is something wrong, answer "yes" and indicate what's wrong. If nothing is wrong, answer "no; this one is correct." At the end of this exercise you will find the answers.

yes 1. People in a ~~good~~ _bad_ mood are so wrapped up in their ~~success~~ _failure_ that it lowers their willingness to help a stranger.

yes 2. Infants are generally ~~not~~ able to communicate information via facial expressions to their caregivers.

_no_ 3. People who exaggerate their facial responsiveness while watching a humorous monologue rate the monologue to be funnier than people who do not exaggerate.

no, correct

4. People in need of aid who stared at passersby were more likely to receive aid than people who didn't stare.

yes

5. Females transmit nonverbal messages more effectively ~~than males, but males~~ *and* are better receivers.

yes

6. The best predictor of how good a person is at sending nonverbal messages is his/her ~~biological sex.~~ *femininity or masculinity*

7. A study suggests that when husbands accurately transmit nonverbal messages, their wives voice fewer complaints.

yes

8. We acquire especially useful information about others from behavior that has ~~many~~ *only one* potential ~~reasons~~ supporting its occurrence.

no, correct

9. We are likely to attribute another person's behavior to external causes when consensus is high, consistency is high, and distinctiveness is high.

yes ;

10. In Schachter and Singer's study, subjects given the epinephrine injection and informed about what side effects to expect were ~~especially~~ likely to model their behavior after the confederate. *less*   *The uninformed were more likely.*

Is Something Wrong Here? Answers

1. Yes; most people seem more willing to do simple favors when in a good mood. (41)

2. Yes; facial expressions are useful vehicles of communication for infants. (45)

3. No; this one is correct. (46)

4. No; this one is correct. (48)

5. Yes; females are better transmitters and receivers. (52)

6. Yes; the best predictor is their "masculinity/femininity," regardless of biological sex. (52)

7. ~~No; this one is correct. (54)~~
   Yes ;

8. Yes; with many potential reasons, we don't know which to hold accountable. (56)

9. No; this one is correct. (58)

10. Yes; it is the underlined subjects, with no explanation for what's happening, who are influenced by the confederate. (74)

20

<u>True-False</u>

Indicate whether each of the following statements is true or false. Correct answers are at the end of the exercise.

1. The number of emotions that are represented by their own distinct facial expressions is six.   *T*

2. The fact that only six emotions are represented by distinct facial expressions means that we are capable of expressing only six different emotional expressions.   *F*

3. People in different cultures express various emotions quite differently from one another.   *F*

4. There is evidence to support the notion that facial expressions have universal meaning.   *T*

5. Men and women are generally equally capable when it comes to the use of nonverbal cues.   *F*

6. It is generally recognized that the superiority of women over men in the ability to use nonverbal cues is due to innate factors.   *F*

7. When other people stare at us, we generally interpret it as a sign that they like us.   *F*

8. The text states that the effect of a stare is always negative.   *F*

9. Wimer and Kelley (1982) concluded that the only dimension on which our causal attributions differ is the internal-external dimension.   *F*

10. When individuals are provided with rewards for an activity that they already find enjoyable, their enjoyment of the activity increases.   *F*

<u>True-False Answers</u>

1. True (42)

2. False; while there <u>are</u> six distinct facial expressions, we are capable of expressing more than six emotions. This is possible because the six facial expressions occur in <u>combinations</u> and also vary in <u>intensity</u>.   (42)

3. False; in fact, people show the same basic facial expressions.
(42)

4. True (43)

21

5. False; studies have consistently shown women to be superior to men, both in transmitting and receiving nonverbal information. (52)

6. False; it appears that the differences stem from child-rearing practices. (52)

7. False; staring usually produces unpleasant feelings in us and is seen as a sign of hostility. (48)

8. False; positive effects are sometimes produced, the best example being the increased aid offered to a person in need of help when that person stares at passersby. (48)

9. False; while the familiar internal-external dimension was found, they also found attributions to vary on the other dimensions shown in Table 2-1. (62)

10. False; when rewards are provided, enjoyment often decreases because the individual now perceives himself to be doing it for the reward. (72)

Fill-in-the-Blanks

Complete the following statements by filling in the blanks with correct information. The answers are at the end of this exercise.

1. The single most important source of information about others' current feelings is _verbal communication_.

2. While particular facial expressions may universally portray particular emotions, whether the emotion is actually expressed in a particular situation may depend on the _display rules_ for the culture.

3. The age at which babies begin to show discrete, recognizable facial expressions that reflect their emotional states is _1-2 months_.

4. In general, we interpret a high level of eye contact from another person as a sign of _friendliness_.

5. When another person gazes at us in a continuous manner and maintains such contact regardless of actions on our part, the person may be said to be _staring_.

22

6. The type of gesture that carries a specific meaning within a particular culture is the _____emblem_____.

7. The process by which we infer the stable characteristics of others by observing their overt actions and the circumstances under which these actions occur is _____attribution_____.

8. To the extent that another person's actions are shaped by _____external_____ causes, they cannot be used as grounds for inferring that person's motives or traits.

9. The basic task we face in making a causal attribution is determining whether a behavior is caused by _____internal_____ or _____external_____ causes.

10. We tend to see our own behavior as stemming largely from _____situations_____; we tend to see the behavior of others as stemming largely from _____internal dispositions_____.

11. Among players and coaches of major sports teams, it seems that _____successes_____ are accounted for in terms of internal causes, while _____failures_____ are accounted for in terms of external causes.

12. The _____ego-defensive_____ explanation for the self-serving bias says we enhance our feelings about ourselves by taking credit for positive outcomes and denying responsibility for negative outcomes.

13. The _____self-presentation_____ explanation for the self-serving bias suggests that our desire to appear in a favorable light to others is what motivates self-serving bias.

14. _____Bem's self perception theory_____ states that we come to know our own attitudes, emotions, and feelings by observing our own behavior and the circumstances under which it occurs.

23

15. A potential disadvantage in the use of rewards is that the

    intrinsic motivation of the recipient may be

    reduced.

Fill-in-the-Blanks Answers

1. what they verbally tell us (41)
2. display rules (44)
3. about one to two months (44)
4. friendliness (48)
5. staring (48)
6. emblem (49)
7. attribution (54)
8. external (57)
9. internal; external (57)
10. situational factors; internal dispositions or traits (64)
11. wins; losses (66)
12. ego-defensive (66)
13. self-presentation (66)
14. Bem's self-perception theory (71)
15. intrinsic (72)

Multiple Choice

1. When we seek to determine the effect of moods, feelings, and
   emotions on behavior, we are dealing with _____ causes;
   attribution deals with the effect of _____ causes.
   a. temporary; more lasting   c. situational; more personal
   b. permanent; more temporary   d. personal; more environmental

   a

2. Which of the following is <u>not</u> one of the emotions represented by a
   distinct facial expression?
   a. happiness   c. anger
   b. surprise   d. suspicion

   d

3. The ability to "read" other peoples' facial expressions seems to
   be
   a. dependent on learning, since each culture has its own meaning
      for each expression
   b. dependent on learning, since only people who know each other
      are able to do it
   c. uniquely associated with Americans
   d. universal
   e. both a and b

   d

4. <u>Statement A.</u> Only a highly trained expert, using the Facial
   Expression Scoring Manual, is able to determine what emotion a
   baby's face is portraying.
   <u>Statement B.</u> Facial expressions are generally a useful means
   for infants to transmit information to their caregivers.
   a. both statements are true
   b. both statements are false
   c. statement A is true; statement B is false
   d. statement B is true; statement A is false

   d

5. Among animals stares are often
   a. a preliminary in reproductive behavior
   b. a sign of hostility or anger
   c. a sign of liking
   d. both c and d

   b

6. Emblems convey
   a. that a person is emotionally aroused
   b. a low level of emotional arousal
   c. a specific meaning within a given culture
   d. that the person is ill-at-ease
   e. both a and d

   c

7. With regard to sex differences in the use of nonverbal cues,
   research suggests that
   a. females are superior to males
   b. males are superior to females
   c. males and females are not different
   d. females transmit messages more effectively, but males are
      better receivers
   e. males transmit messages more effectively, but females are
      better receivers

   a

25

8. Which of the following statements is false?
    a. the better wives' ability to read poorly encoded nonverbal messages from their husbands, the fewer complaints about the relationship from both partners
    b. the more accurate the wives in transmitting nonverbal messages, the fewer the complaints voiced by their husbands
    c. the more accurate the husbands in transmitting nonverbal messages, the fewer the complaints voiced by their wives
    d. none are false (i.e., all are true)

9. We are more likely to reach correspondent inferences about others when their behavior
    a. is seen to be socially desirable and to have occurred by choice
    b. is seen to be socially undesirable and to have occurred by choice
    c. is seen to be socially desirable and to have occurred without choice
    d. is seen to be socially undesirable and to have occurred without choice

10. To the extent that another person's actions are shaped by_____ causes, they do not allow one to infer that person's motives or traits.
    a. external   c. objective
    b. internal   d. subjective

11. We are likely to attribute another person's behavior to external causes when consensus is _____, consistency is _____, and distinctiveness is _____.
    a. high; high; high   c. low; high; low
    b. low; low; low   d. high; low; high

12. The person who is a cognitive miser tends to explain the fact that a person laughs at a funny joke
    a. on the basis of consensus information only
    b   by either consensus, distinctiveness, or consistency information, depending on which is most easily obtained
    c. in terms of the joke, based on past experience
    d. by discounting complicated information
    e. both b and d

13. Statement A. The discounting and augmenting principles apply mainly to situations in which we have the opportunity to observe a person's behavior in several situations and at different times.
    Statement B. Wimer and Kelley (1982) concluded that the only dimension on which our causal attributions differ is the internal-external dimension.
    a. both statements are true
    b. both statements are false
    c. statement A is true; statement B is false
    d. statement A is false; statement B is true

14. Whose behavior of tripping and falling on the sidewalk are we more likely to attribute to the "clumsiness" of the person? b
    a. our own, but only if someone sees us fall
    b. another person's
    c. our own, but only when no one sees us fall
    d. either a or c, since it doesn't matter whether we are seen or not
    e. there is no difference between any of the above alternatives

15. Among players and coaches of major sports teams, Lau and Russell a (1980) found that_____ were accounted for in terms of internal causes, while _____ were more likely to be accounted for externally.
    a. wins; losses
    b. losses; wins
    c. their own mistakes; the other team's mistakes
    d. the other team's mistakes; their own mistakes

Multiple Choice Answers

1.	a (41)	9.	b (56)
2.	d (42)	10.	a (57)
3.	d (44)	11.	a (60)
4.	d (45)	12.	c (62)
5.	b (48)	13.	b (64)
6.	c (49)	14.	b (66)
7.	a (52)	15.	a
8.	c (54)		

Just for Fun: Some Additional Readings

Marlatt, G.A. and Rohsenow, D.J. The think-drink effect. _Psychology Today_, December, 1981, pp. 61 ff. It follows from Schachter's theory of emotion that people will act in stereotyped ways when they _think_ they're drinking alcohol--even when it's tonic water in their glasses.

Rosenthal, Robert et al. Body talk and tone of voice: The language without words. _Psychology Today_, September, 1974, pp. 64 ff. A visual test is discussed that measures sensitivity to nonverbal messages. Wome are better at analyzing nonverbal messages than men.

Greene, David and Lepper, Mark R. Intrinsic motivation: How to turn play into work. _Psychology Today_, September, 1974, pp. 49-52. A brief introduction to the Greene and Lepper's well-known work on how rewards can undermine intrinsic motivation.

Beier, Ernst G. Nonverbal communication: How we send emotional messages. _Psychology Today_, October, 1974, pp. 52 ff. Our faces, our intonations, the ways we hold our bodies often send emotional messages we don't intend.

Hall, Elizabeth T. How cultures collide. _Psychology Today_, August, 1976. In an interview with Edward T. Hall, nonverbal behavior and how it is culturally determined is discussed.

CHAPTER 3

SOCIAL COGNITION: THINKING ABOUT (AND MAKING
SENSE OF) THE SOCIAL WORLD

Objectives

1. Compare and contrast social perception and social cognition. *they are related; social cognition is broader and deals with how we think about others not only how we understand their behavior*

2. Summarize the methods used by social psychologists to measure attention, memory, inference, and social cognition processes. *measure time spent → decision time → computer simulation looking at objects information on test recall structural equations*

3. Summarize the nature, origins, and development of social schemata. *richly interconnected networks of information relevant to various concepts abstracted from experience*

4. Define each of the following types of schemata: prototypes, *single best example* role schemata, person schemata, self-schemata, and event *based on age, sex, race etc.* schemata (or scripts). *when applied to specific persons → when applied to self → normal course of events in various familiar settings.*

5. Summarize the effect that social schemata have on our perception of others' behavior. *we more or less induce the persons around us to behave in ways that confirm our expectations*

6. Summarize the effect that schemata have on selective attention. *schemata are hard to change and will often determine what we pay attention to ie those things that support our schemata*

7. Summarize the effect that schemata have on our memory about others. *Powerful effect that enables us to remember only those characteristics that fit the schemata*

8. Summarize the effects of salience and vividness on attention. *salience (those things which are different from others) has the most effect while vividness is somewhat weaker*

9. List the effects that attention has on social cognition. *perception of causality — causes more extreme evaluations*

10. What effects are produced by self-focused attention (i.e. objective self-awareness)? *causes an increase in consistency between attitudes and values and overt behavior*

11. Summarize the contents of person memory. *appearance, behavior, traits*

12. Describe how being instructed to remember details vs. to form an overall impression affects person memory. *overall impression causes better organization and thereby better recall.*

13. Describe the priming produced by accessible categories. *recent use of a particular category will "prime" an individual memory for characteristics that are accessible from that same category*

14. How do individual differences in visual imagery affect person memory? *the ability to form vivid images greatly effects the ability of a person to recall what has impressed them*

15. How does the overemphasizing of extreme cases affect social inference? *by exaggerating the frequency that we perceive the social behavior to occur*

16. How does ignoring information about typicality affect social inference? *it will interpret atypical behavior as a norm*

17. Describe the illusory correlation. *when we expect a covariation between to variables, we often exaggerate the correlation beyond its true value*

18. Summarize the impact of the availability heuristic and of the representativeness heuristic on social inference. *both bias social inferences by taking short cuts. importance is based on availability according to relevant importance*

19. Compare adding, simple averaging, and weighted averaging views of impression formation. ✓ *adding up + or - ; by comparing + to - ; takes into account relative importance of + + -*

20. List the factors that determine the weight given a bit of information. *credibility, information first obtained (first impressions), weight - more than +*

21. How does the evaluator's disposition affect his rating of others? *by influencing first impressions either + or -*

22. What cognitive stages does one go through in forming an impression? *initial encoding, elaborative encoding, integration, decision*

23. How are affect and cognition related? How does mood affect memory? *possibly by a shared mechanism in our motor system. by interrupting memory; by influencing our perceptions when memories are formed; by influencing what type of things we remember*

Who Done It?

Credit each of the concepts, theories, critical studies or important ideas listed below to the person or persons associated with each (e.g., item: Id-Ego-Superego; associated person: Freud). Answers are on the next page.

1. study demonstrating that we perceive behavior of white and black children quite differently *Sager & Schofield*

2. study showing that subjects prefer feedback that confirms their self-concepts *Swann & Read*

3. study showing that schema-consistent information regarding another person is easier to recall than schema-inconsistent information *Cohen*

4. study demonstrating that being told to form an over-all impression facilitates person memory *Hamilton, Katz, Leirer*

5. study showing that priming affects what we remember about a person *Snull & Wyer*

30

6. study showing that a brutal prison guard affects our attitude toward all prison guards, even if the brutal guard is "atypical" *Hamill, Wilson, & Nisbett*

7. proposed model dividing impression formation into four distinct phases *Burnstein & Schul*

8. study showing that mood-consistent facial expressions facilitate recall *Laird, et al*

Who Done It? Answers

1. Sagar and Schofield (93) *study with black vs white children & aggression*
2. Swann and Read (95) *confirming of self-schemata*
3. Cohen (96) *schema-consistent info easier to recall waitress/librarian*
4. Hamilton, Katz, and Leirer (103) *overall impression forms better memory*
5. Srull and Wyer (105) *priming effects recall*
6. Hamill, Wilson, and Nisbett (109) *effect of typicality on inference*
7. Burnstein and Schul (115) *4 phase model of impression formation*
8. Laird, et al. (117) *effect of mood-consistent facial expressions on recall*

Define

Each of the critical concepts listed below have been defined in your textbook. For each provide the definition. Answers are on the next page.

1. social cognition : *the thoughts we have about ourselves & others based on past experience, education, etc*

2. schemata : *networks of information formed by past experience*

3. category accessibility : *the ease with which we bring into awareness various areas of our memory*

4. covariation : *the degree in which changes in one factor bring about changes in another*

5. illusory correlation : *a mistaken perception of co-variation between two elements*

6. the availability heuristic : *the idea that the information which easily comes to mind is the important information relative to understanding a given social situation*

7. cognition : *thought*

8. affect : *emotion*

31

Definitions

[handwritten margin notes: Social Cognition, Schemata, Category accessibility, Co-variation, illusory correlation, the availability heuristic, cognition, affect]

1. research area dealing with how we think about others and attempt to make sense out of the social world (84)

2. networks of information built up through past experience (the singular of this word is schema) (89)

3. ease with which we can recall or bring into awareness various portions of our memory (104)

4. degree to which changes in one factor are accompanied by changes in a second factor (108)

5. the <u>mistaken</u> perception that there is covariation between two factors (109)

6. the notion that if we can readily remember information, then it is important or occurs frequently; we use this principle in making social inferences (110)

7. thought (116)

8. feeling (116)

Matching

Match each concept or idea on the left with an identifying phrase, word or sentence on the right. Answers are at the bottom of this page.

A. recall and recognition
B. typicality
C. ignoring typicality
D. use of heuristics
E. primacy effect
F. Ebenezer Scrooge syndrome
G. objective self-awareness

C 1. is a social inference bias
F 2. opposite of Pollyana syndrome
E 3. produces strong first impression
A 4. measures of memory
B 5. baserate information
G 6. produced by self-focused attention
D 7. shows we're cognitive misers

Is Something Wrong Here?

For each statement below indicate what is wrong about the statement, if anything. If there _is_ something wrong, answer "yes" and indicate what's wrong. If nothing is wrong, answer "no; this one is correct." At the end of this exercise you will find the answers.

1. When an experimenter exposes a subject to several stimuli simultaneously and measures the amount of time spent looking at each, decision time is what's being measured.
   yes _attention is being measured_

2. Computer simulation and structural equations are used to determine the nature of social cognition processes.
   _no_

3. Our schemata are _not_ easily modified, _when_ when we receive evidence that contradicts them.
   yes

4. When asked to describe another person, most people begin with physical appearance.
   _no_

5. A person told to remember as many details as possible is _not_ able to recall more information about a person she has just met than a person told to form an over-all impression.
   yes _Over all impression seems to better organize information for recall_

6. The priming effect in Srull and Wyer's (1980) study was at its maximum immediately after seeing the information, and then declined. _It seemed to be strongest after a week_
   yes

7. Even after we have decided that some belief is false it may continue to influence our thought because of its availability.
   _no_

8. The text suggests that making important social decisions in group settings decreases the errors in the social inference process.
   _no_

9. Zajonc and Markus (1983) speculate that affect and cognition are linked through their joint representation in our motor system.
   _no_

10. Subjects who tried to recall amusing stories by Woody Allen showed better recall when they suppressed their emotional reaction. _Their recall was better when they exaggerated their emotional reaction_
   yes

Is Something Wrong Here? Answers

1. Yes; attention-eliciting value of the stimuli is probably what's being measured. (86)

2. No; this one is correct. (87)

3. Yes; we tend to discount contradictory evidence and thereby keep our schemata intact. (92)

4. No; this one is correct. (101)

33

5. Yes; instructions to form an overall impression leads to greater recall of details because it benefits organization.
(102)

6. Yes; surprisingly, the priming effect was greater after seven days than it had been immediately. (105)

7. No; this one is correct. (112)

8. No; this one is correct. (113)

9. No; this one is correct. (118)

10. Yes; the best recall occurred when they smiled during recall, especially if they actually experienced a mood that matched the smile. (117)

True-False

Indicate whether each of the following statements is true or false. Correct answers are at the end of the exercise.

F 1. Research in social cognition has developed almost entirely within social psychology.

F 2. The text states that the reason we can't study cognitive processes by simply having people report these to us is that people try to conceal their cognitive processes.

F 3. It was found that white children perceived a black child's actions as meaner, while black children perceived a white child's actions as meaner.

T 4. People seem to prefer information about themselves that is consistent with their own self-schemata.

T 5. Subjects recall schema-consistent information more readily than schema-inconsistent information.

F 6. The impact of salience on attention seems to be weaker and less consistent than that of vividness.

T 7. Subjects who read that imaginary strangers had committed extreme crimes also estimated that crime frequency was high for these individuals.

F 8. When subjects watched a prison guard "being interviewed," their attitudes about prison guards were affected only when this particular guard was said to be typical.

F 9. We attach greater weight to positive information about others than we do to negative information.

34

T 10. The speed of initial encoding should depend heavily on the
number of traits describing the other person.

F 11. The speed of initial encoding should depend heavily on the
amount of inconsistency between the traits presented.

True-False Answers

1. False; in fact, research in social cognition has been stimulated
largely by developments outside social psychology. (85)

2. False; it is argued that people are simply too dimly aware of
cognitive processes to report them. (86)

3. False; Sagar and Schofield (1980) found that a black child's
actions were perceived to be meaner by both black and white
children. (93)

4. True   (94)

5. True   (96)

6. False; in fact, <u>vividness</u> has less impact.   (99)

7. True   (107)

8. False; the guard's statements influenced subjects' attitudes
regardless of typicality information. (108)

9. False; negative information is weighted more heavily. (114)

10. True   (118)

11. False; the speed of <u>integration</u> is affected by inconsistency
between traits. (119)

Fill-in-the-Blanks

Complete the following statements by filling in the blanks with
correct information. The answers are at the end of this exercise.

1. A schema which identifies the best single example of a particular

category is called a __*prototype*__ .

2. Schemata referring to members of ethnic, racial, or age-related

groups are __*role-schemata*__ .

35

3. A person's schema regarding what constitutes a particular personality characteristic is a _person schema_.

4. The term that refers to our stable conception of our own personality is _self-schemata_.

5. On the basis of past experience, I have firm expectations regarding the usual course of events when a person takes a trip by airplane. These expectations are _event schema or scripts_.

6. The fact that novel, colorful, or otherwise unusual stimuli capture our attention illustrates the effect of _salience_ on attention.

7. The term that refers to the emotion-provoking, imagery-producing properties of a stimulus is _vividness_.

8. When conditions make a particular memory category accessible so that recall of information relating to the category is enhanced, this is called a _priming_ effect.

9. The term that refers to a basic rule or principle used to simplify the social inference process is _heuristic_.

10. The term that describes the fact that certain traits or behaviors generally occur together, such that the presence of one implies the presence of the other is _co-variation_.

11. When a person decides whether someone has a particular trait based on how easily instances of such behavior can be recalled, he is using the _availability_ heuristic to make the decision.

12. To determine whether someone is a teacher, I compare his traits to the "average" teacher. I am using the _representativeness_ heuristic.

13. The most accurate picture of how we actually combine information about others in forming an overall impression is provided by the _weighted averaging_ model.

14. List the four stages of the impression formation process in their correct order: 1) _initial encoding_ ; 2) _elaborative encoding_ ; 3) _integration_ ; 4) _decision_ .

15. In the _initial encoding_ phase, information about another person is brought from outside and transformed into our cognitive system.

16. During the _elaborative encoding_ phase, social information is linked to various social schemata that are already present.

Fill-in-the-Blank Answers

1. prototype (89)
2. role schemata (89)
3. person schema (90)
4. self-schemata (90)
5. event schemata or scripts (91)
6. salience (97)
7. vividness (98)
8. priming (104)
9. heuristic (110)
10. co-variation (108)
11. availability (110)
12. representativeness (111)
13. weighted averaging (114)
14. initial encoding; elaborative encoding; integration; decision (115)
15. initial encoding (115)
16. elaborative encoding (118)

Multiple Choice

a 1. Schemata are:
   a. cognitive structures built up through experience which influence the processing of new information
   b. patterns of social behavior that individuals follow in a given culture
   c. an important form of nonverbal cues
   d. a modern technique used by dentists to treat tooth decay

b 2. A schema which identifies the best single example of a particular category is called a
   a. role schema   c. script
   b. prototype   d. person schema

d 3. In their study dealing with the effects of schemata on perception, Sagar and Schofield (1980) found that
   a. black children's actions were perceived as meaner than white children's actions by black subjects
   b. black children's actions were perceived as meaner than white children's actions by white subjects
   c. white children's actions were perceived as meaner than black children's actions by black subjects
   d. a and b
   e. b and c

a 4. Which summarizes the effect of schema on memory in the Cohen (1981) study?
   a. being told that a woman was a waitress led subjects to recall waitress-relevant information
   b. given waitress-relevant information, subjects concluded the woman was a waitress
   c. subjects assumed women were waitresses, since they were more frequently found than librarians
   d. schema-inconsistent information was more easily recalled

c 5. Which is true?
   a. the attention-eliciting property of stimuli is determined solely by their salience and vividness
   b. vividness more strongly affects attention than salience
   c. we may consciously choose to direct our attention to certain aspects of the social world rather than to others
   d. all are true

b 6. We will tend to withdraw from self-focused attention
   a. whenever we compare our behavior with our own standards
   b. when the adjustment process is no longer feasible
   c. when our behavior exceeds our own standards
   d. when our behavior falls short of our own standards

38

7. Persons told to form an overall impression of a stranger
   a. were able to recall relatively few specific items of information about the stranger
   b. were able to recall more items of information than persons told to memorize the information exactly
   c. recalled the same amount of information as persons told to memorize the information exactly
   d. were more favorable in their judgments than persons who memorized

8. Do individuals differ in terms of the accessibility of various memory categories? Does the accessibility of memory categories affect the impressions people form?
   a. yes, yes   c. no, yes
   b. yes, no   d. no, no

9. What happens when we are informed of a small number of extreme cases regarding another person?
   a. we are not unduly affected by these cases
   b. these cases are usually discounted
   c. these cases are usually discounted because we tend to find them unbelievable
   d. these cases often have an unduly large impact

10. Suppose that I assume a covariation between being an athlete and being dumb. The notion of illusory correlation suggests that
   a. because I anticipate such a relationship, I will overestimate it
   b. because I anticipate such a relationship, I will underestimate it
   c. I will assess the relationship accurately because of my interest in it
   d. it is always wrong to assume that variables are related

11. When my new neighbor walks out of his apartment with a whistle around his neck, carrying a clipboard and a basketball, I conclude that he's a coach. My conclusion is based on
   a. the availability heuristic   c. baserate information
   b. the representativeness   d. visual imagery
      heuristic

12. The greater the amount of positive input we have about a person, the more favorable our final impression. This prediction follows from the _____ model of impression formation
   a. adding   c. weighted averaging
   b. simple averaging   d. cognitive algebra

13. A primacy effect refers to our tendency to
   a. assign greater weight to information we obtain first
   b. assign greater weight to information relating to extreme behavior
   c. assign greater weight to negative than to positive information about others
   d. assign greater weight to information coming from a credible source

39

C 14. During the _____ phase, social information is linked to various social schemata that are already present.
   a. initial encoding c. elaborative encoding
   b. integration d. decision

b 15. Subjects who tried to recall amusing stories by Woody Allen showed better recall
   a. than subjects trying to recall anger-provoking editorials
   b. when smiling than when frowning
   c. when frowning than when smiling
   d. when they suppressed their emotional reactions

b 16. Zajonc and Markus (1983) speculate that affect and cognition are linked through
   a. a genetic mechanism
   b. their joint representation in our motor system
   c. their joint representation in our cognitive system
   d. a cultural mechanism unique to Americans

<u>Multiple Choice Answers</u>

1. a (86)   9. d (107)
2. b (89)   10. a (109)
3. d (93)   11. b (111)
4. a (96)   12. a (113)
5. c (99)   13. a (114)
6. b (101) 14. c (118)
7. b (103) 15. b (118)
8. a (105) 16. b (118)

Just for Fun: Some Additional Readings

Slovic, P. Fischhoff, Lichtenstein, S. Risky assumptions. Psychology Today, June, 1980. Erroneous thought is the tip of the
iceberg. These researchers show how erroneous attributions and
other kinds of human error can get us into hot water à la Three
Mile Island.

Parlee, M. Conversational politics. Psychology Today, May, 1979.
Erhummmm, uh....like....you know....really. Start this way and
you have already made a bad impression. What kind of person
you are perceived to be may depend on how you carry on a conversation (or fail to do so).

Harre, R. What's in a nickname? Psychology Today, January, 1980.
Harre argues that children's nicknames represent a way of marking
status hierarchies and norms and learning to function as adults.

Reed, Julia A. You are what you wear. Human Behavior, July, 1974.
The brief article shows a relationship between women's choice of
clothes and aspects of their personalities.

CHAPTER 4

ATTITUDES AND ATTITUDE CHANGE:

REACTIONS TO THE SOCIAL WORLD

Objectives

1. What is the definition of an attitude and why are attitudes of interest?

2. Explain the role of instrumental conditioning, modeling, and direct experience in the development of attitudes.

3. Contrast informal self-reports with the Likert Scaling technique and other questionnaire methods.

4. Describe how the bogus pipeline and unobtrusive measures are used to improve the accuracy of attitude measurement.

5. Describe how the communicator's attractiveness, speed of talking, expertise, and intentions affect attitude change.

6. Discuss person-positivity bias.

7. Under what conditions are fear communications effective in changing attitudes? *strong appeals, danger must be perceived as real, warning must be perceived as actually working to avoid danger.*

8. Summarize the role of recipients' self-schemata in attitude change. *the more relevant an appeal to ones self-schemata the more effective*

9. How are personality factors and memory of relevant information related to susceptibility to persuasion? *that who can bring attitude relevant beliefs to mind readily are less susceptible*

10. Summarize the role played by the right vs. left brain hemisphere as we respond to persuasive messages. *left is analytical - right is more emotion based, global*

11. Describe the various conditions under which the mere-exposure effect occurs and the two limitations. *frequent exposure to wide range of stimuli negative as well as positive stimuli, unconsciously / stimuli must be complex*

12. Describe how reactance, forewarning, and inoculation create resistance to persuasion. *protecting on personal freedom* *only to a point*

43

1. add consonant elements
2. reduce or minimize the importance of some cognitive elements involved
3. alter one or both of the cognitive elements producing the dissonance

13. What are the basic assumptions of dissonance theory?
    a) List the ways in which dissonance can be reduced following attitude-discrepant behavior.
    b) What is meant by "selecting the path of least resistance"? *the element least resistant to change will be altered*

14. When persons receive rewards for engaging in attitude-discrepant behavior, what level of reward produces the most attitude change? *the smallest amount that will engage the behavior*

15. What three conditions seem to be necessary to produce the "less-leads-to-more" effect? *1) freedom to choose 2) small reward 3) payment must be well-deserved pay not a bribe*

16. Describe the attitude change that occurs in response to the expenditure of effort. *the greater the expenditure of effort the more attitude change*

17. Summarize the findings on how alcohol consumption affects subsequent dissonance-caused attitude change.

18. Describe how attitude strength, attitude specificity, and attitude relevance affect whether we will translate our attitudes into behavior.
specific attitudes predict behavior better than global ones
attitudes that affect outcomes are better predictors of behavior than attitudes that do not

Who Done It?

strong attitudes predict behavior more successfully than weak ones

Credit each of the concepts, theories, critical studies or important ideas listed below to the person or persons associated with each (e.g., item: Id-Ego-Superego; associated person: Freud). Answers are on the next page.

1. study suggesting that attitudes formed through direct experience are stronger *Fazio, et al.*

2. study suggesting that how we perceive communicator's motives depends on whether he takes an expected or an unexpected position *Wood & Eagly*

3. study suggesting that messages that match one's self-schemata are more persuasive *Cacioppo*

4. study suggesting that brain hemisphere activity is related to degree of polarized thought *Cacioppo*

5. author of cognitive dissonance theory *Festinger*

6. study suggesting that alcohol consumption stops the usual dissonance-produced shifts in attitude *Steele, Southwick, & Critchlow*

7. study suggesting that one's vested interest is a strong determinant of the attitude-behavior link *Sivacek & Crano*

44

Who Done It Answers

1. Fazio, et al. (129)
2. Wood and Eagly (140)
3. Cacioppo, Petty, and Sidera (142)
4. Cacioppo, Petty, and Quintanar (146)
5. Festinger (151)
6. Steele, Southwick, and Critchlow (160)
7. Sivacek and Crano (163)

Define

Each of the critical concepts listed below have been defined in your textbook. For each provide the definition. Answers are on the next page.

1. attitude— *our lasting feelings, beliefs, & behavior tendencies with respect to an object*

2. Likert scale *the most frequently used self-report scale in which subjects express their extent of agreement with relevant statements*

3. bogus pipeline — *a technique used to induce truthfulness of answers to questions by making subjects believe they are attached to a machine that can tell when they are lying*

4. reactance — *the unpleasant state that occurs when one believes their personal freedom is threatened*

5. inoculation — *a technique used to increase ability to resist influence techniques whereby the person is exposed to arguments against his belief which are then refuted*

6. cognitive dissonance *the unpleasant state that arises when a person is faced with inconsistency between attitudes & behavior, or between attitudes*

7. attitude-discrepant behavior — *acting in a way that is contrary to the beliefs or feelings one holds*

8. "less-leads-to-more" effect — *small rewards that illicit attitude-discrepant behavior lead to greater changes in attitude than do large rewards*

Matching

Match each concept or idea on the left with an identifying phrase, word or sentence on the right. Answers are on the next page.

A. forced compliance situation
B. new consonant element
C. attitudes
D. attitude scale
E. refutational defense
F. strong attitudes
G. attitude relevance
H. imagining contact

D 1. same as questionnaire
G 2. basis for vested interest
A 3. attitude-discrepant behavior occurs here
B 4. reduces dissonance
C 5. clusters of feelings, beliefs, and behavior tendencies
E 6. best inoculator
F 7. readily accessed from memory
H 8. successful "therapy" for snake phobia

Definitions

1. our lasting feelings, beliefs, and behavior tendencies with respect to an object (126)

2. the most frequently used self-report scale, in which subjects express their extent of agreement with relevant statements (132)

3. method for measuring attitudes in which subjects are induced to be more truthful by being led to believe that a machine can measure their true beliefs (133)

4. the unpleasant state that occurs when one feels his personal freedom threatened (152)

5. a technique that increases one's ability to resist influence attempts; the person is exposed to arguments against his beliefs and then these arguments are refuted (153)

6. the unpleasant state that occurs when the person is faced with inconsistency between attitudes and behavior, or between attitudes (151)

7. acting in a way that is inconsistent with one's feeling or belief (150)

8. refers to the dissonance finding in the attitude-discrepant behavior situation; small rewards for engaging in attitude discrepant behavior are associated with large amounts of attitude change. (157)

Matching Answers

1.	D (131)	5. C	(126)
2.	G (163)	6. E	(153)
3.	A (155)	7. F	(159)
4.	B (151)	8. H	(158)

Is Something Wrong Here?

For each statement below indicate what is wrong about the statement, if anything. If there is something wrong, answer "Yes" and indicate what's wrong. If nothing is wrong, answer "No; this one is correct." At the end of this exercise you will find the answers.

correct
1. Our attitudes seem to be stronger and easier to remember when they are acquired through direct experience.

wrong
2. When asked for their views about important issues where they do not hold clearly formed attitudes, most people reply, "I don't know." *will state their views anyway*

wrong
3. The most common technique used to alter attitudes is the dissonance approach. *persuasive communication*

46

correct

4. A liked communicator is generally more persuasive than disliked ones, unless the liked communicator's appeal stems from some special bias.

wrong *high*

5. Persons who are ~~low~~ in the need for social approval are generally more easily persuaded than persons who are high on this characteristic. *low*

wrong

6. The two circumstances under which the usual frequency of exposure/liking relationship often fails to occur are when complex stimuli are used and when the number of exposures is very large.

correct

7. When subjects perceive that influence attempts are unduly strong, feelings of reactance are often produced.

correct

8. When several avenues of dissonance reduction are available, the path that will actually be selected is the path of least resistance.

wrong *less*

9. In the Festinger and Carlsmith (1959) experiment, the ~~more~~ money subjects were paid to tell another person how interesting a boring experiment was, the more the subjects believed what they had said.

wrong

10. When subjects consumed alcohol after engaging in attitude-discrepant behavior, they displayed even more attitude change than usual. *less*

correct

11. Specific attitudes predict behavior more successfully than global ones.

Is Something Wrong Here? Answers

1. No; this one is correct. (129)

2. Yes; most people state an attitude anyway. (131)

3. Yes; most commonly used is the persuasive communication. (135)

4. No; this one is correct. (137)

5. Yes; persons <u>high</u> in this need are more easily persuaded. (144)

6. This statement is "half right"; however, the relationship fails when <u>simple</u> stimuli are used. (150)

7. No; this one is correct. (152)

8. No; this statement is also correct. (155)

9. Yes, it's the other way around; the <u>less</u> subjects were paid, the more they believed what they had said. (156)

10. Yes; these subjects failed to show the usual dissonance-produced shift in attitude. (160)

11. No; this one is correct. (162)

True-False

Indicate whether each of the following statements is true or false. Correct answers are at the end of the exercise.

F 1. In the Miller, et al. (1976) experiment, the speaker who spoke at a slower than normal rate produced the greatest agreement with his message.

F 2. In order for a communicator to change peoples' attitudes, it is best to argue for a position from which he stands to gain.

F 3. A communicator who adopts an unexpected position is perceived to be biased.

T 4. Fear appeals have been effectively used to change peoples' attitudes regarding dental hygiene.

T 5. Research has supported the notion that some people are more easily persuaded than others.

F 6. Wood (1982) found that, when presented with a persuasive communicator, the most attitude change was shown by subjects who could recall many attitude-relevant beliefs and behaviors.

F 7. Subjects with a high level of activity in the right brain hemisphere report thinking both favorable and unfavorable thoughts, regardless of the message content.

F 8. The general finding has been that people react unfavorably to frequently-presented stimuli.

T 9. Negative attitude change often occurs under conditions that arouse reactance.

T 10. When a person engages in an attitude-discrepant behavior and has very good reasons for performing such actions, little dissonance will be produced.

F 11. The amount of dissonance produced when a person engages in attitude-discrepant behavior is at a maximum when rewards are large.

F 12. The goals we evaluate most positively are the ones that were easily attained.

48

True-False Answers

1. False; the speaker who talked faster than normal produced the greatest agreement. (138)

2. False; the speaker who stands to gain will be seen as a biased speaker. When a speaker argues against his own self-interest, he is highly credible. (139)

3. False; unexpected positions are attributed to factual evidence. (140)

4. True. (141)

5. True. (143)

6. False; the most change was shown by those who could recall few beliefs and behaviors because of their inability to form counterarguments. (144)

7. False; right-hemisphere subjects show mostly favorable thoughts with a pro-attitudinal message and mostly unfavorable thoughts with a counterattitudinal message (i.e. they show polarized thought). (147)

8. False; people generally react favorably. (145)

9. True. (152)

10. True. (156)

11. False; the most dissonance occurs when rewards are just sufficient to produce the behavior. (156)

12. False; we evaluate positively the goals we've worked hardest for, in order to justify the effort we've expended. (158)

Fill-in-the-Blanks

Complete the following statements by filling in the blanks with correct information. The answers are at the end of this exercise.

1. When children's attitudes are influenced by hearing someone say "good" every time they make the correct attitude statement, the process involved is _instrumental_ conditioning.

2. When children acquire attitudes simply by observing adults performing various actions, the process involved is called _modeling_ .

49

3. The type of attitude questionnaire in which a subject indicates her response by placing a check mark along a line labeled "Strongly Agree" at one end and "Strongly Disagree" at the other end is a ___Likert___ scale.

4. The technique for measuring attitudes in which subjects are told that they will be hooked up to a machine that can gauge their true opinions by measuring tiny muscle potentials is the ___bogus pipeline___.

5. The method by which we gain information about attitudes indirectly, through careful study of formal records or physical traces of human behavior is called ___unobtrusive measurement___

6. Our tendency to evaluate other persons favorably is called ___person-positivity bias___.

7. The two most important factors determining the credibility of a given communicator are his ___expertness___ and his ___intention___.

8. The impact of persuasive messages can be enhanced by matching them to recipients' cognitive structures or ___schemata___.

9. Activity in the ___left___ brain hemisphere is associated with abstract, logical thought; activity in the ___right___ hemisphere is associated with more global, less analytic thought.

10. The negative state which occurs when our feeling of personal freedom is limited by someone putting undue pressure on us is called ___reactance___.

11. The procedure in which people first are exposed to arguments against their views and then hear these arguments refuted is called ___inoculation___.

12. _____Dissonance_____ theory predicts that the less justifi-

cation we have for engaging in attitude-discrepant behavior,

the more the attitude change that will follow this behavior.

13. The three factors which influence the strength of the attitude/

behavior relationship are: 1)_____attitude strength_____,

2)_____attitude specificity_____ and 3)_____attitude relevance_____.

Fill-in-the-Blanks Answers

1. instrumental (127)
2. modeling   (128)
3. Likert   (132)
4. bogus pipeline (133)
5. unobtrusive measurement (134)
6. person-positivity bias (138)
7. expertness; intentions (139)
8. schemata   (142)
9. left; right (146)
10. reactance (152)
11. inoculation (153)
12. Dissonance (156)
13. attitude strength; attitude specificity; attitude relevance (165)

e 1. Which is/are included in the text's definition of **attitude**?
   a. clusters of feelings
   b. clusters of beliefs
   c. clusters of behavior tendencies
   d. a and c
   e. a, b, and c

b 2. Our attitude toward another person will probably be the strongest
   a. when it is acquired through observation of his behavior to-
      ward someone else
   b. when it is acquired in a face-to-face meeting with this person
   c. when it is acquired by hearing someone describing this person
   d. before we have learned much about the person

d 3. In responding to an item on a Likert scale, a person indicates
   her response by
   a. circling either "strongly agree," "agree," "uncertain," "dis-
      agree," or "strongly disagree"
   b. placing a check mark along a line labeled "Strongly Agree"
      at one end and "Strongly Disagree" at the other
   c. circling a number between -5 and +5 to indicate her extent of
      agreement or disagreement
   d. any of the above

b 4. I can tell that the home team has lost a football game because I
   can see that the seats in the home-crowd section of the stadium
   are wetter (i.e., covered with more tears) than the seats in the
   visitor section. This is an example of:
   a. a useless and invalid conclusion
   b. the use of unobtrusive measures
   c. the experimental approach
   d. a, b, and c
   e. b and c

a 5. Which condition is likely to produce a result unlike the usual
   pattern of results for communicator attractiveness?
   a. a liked communicator's recommendations seem to stem from her
      special interests
   b. a disliked communicator's recommendations seem to stem from
      her special interests
   c. a liked communicator's recommendations stem from external factors
   d. none of the above--liked communicators are always more influen-
      tial than disliked communicators

d 6. It seems that a fast rate of speech suggests all of the following,
   except
   a. heightened arousal   c. a knowledgeable speaker
   b. deep conviction   d. that the speaker should be
                                   mistrusted

7. According to a recent study by Wood and Eagly (1981), a communicator who adopts an
   a. expected position is perceived as unbiased, and persuasion is enhanced
   b. expected position is perceived as unbiased, but persuasion is reduced
   c. unexpected position is perceived as biased, and persuasion is reduced
   d. unexpected position is perceived as unbiased, and persuasion is enhanced

8. A problem in tailoring a message so that it will fit the self-schemata of the members of a given audience is
   a. it's not clear that attitude change will be affected by tailoring
   b. people resent messages that are relevant to their self-schemata
   c. it is unethical
   d. it is difficult to assess the self-schemata of audience members

9. Subjects who have a high level of activity in the right brain hemisphere
   a. report thinking mostly favorable thoughts about a pro-attitudinal message
   b. report thinking mostly unfavorable thoughts about a counter-attitudinal message
   c. report thinking both favorable and unfavorable thoughts about most messages
   d. both a and b

10. The unpleasant, negative reaction which occurs when we perceive that someone is trying to limit our personal freedom is called
    a. dissonance   d. inoculation
    b. reactance   e. fogging
    c. discrepancy

11. Which of the following techniques was not mentioned in the text as a means for resisting persuasion?
    a. reactance   c. discounting
    b. forewarning   d. inoculation

12. When a person performs an attitude-discrepant action, the amount of dissonance will be at a maximum when rewards for the actions are
    a. much greater than would be needed to induce the action
    b. just barely sufficient to induce the action
    c. so small that the action fails to occur
    d. used in combination with punishments

13. If we expend much effort in attaining some goal
    a. we will tend to evaluate the goal positively
    b. we will tend to evaluate the goal negatively
    c. and evaluate it negatively, little dissonance will be aroused
    d. and evaluate it negatively, dissonance will be aroused
    e. both a and d

53

14. Do attitudes shape overt behavior?
    a. yes
    b. no
    c. sometimes yes, sometimes no
    d. the question is unanswerable

15. The subjects most willing to campaign against the proposed new law raising the drinking age in Michigan were
    a. those the least affected by it
    b. those who would be moderately affected
    c. those the most affected by it
    d. those without any vested interest

16. Which is <u>not</u> one of the factors influencing the strength of the attitude/behavior relationship?
    a. attitude strength
    b. attitude consonance
    c. attitude specificity
    d. attitude relevance

Multiple Choice Answers

1. e (126)	9. d (146)
2. b (129)	10. b (152)
3. d (132)	11. c (153)
4. b (134)	12. b (155)
5. a (137)	13. e (158)
6. d (138)	14. c (159)
7. d (140)	15. c (163)
8. d (143)	16. b (163)

Just for Fun: Some Additional Readings

Moine, D.J. To trust, perchance to buy. Psychology Today, August,
    1982, pp. 51 ff. Suggests that the best persuaders mirror the
    customer's thoughts, tone of voice, speech tempo, and mood.

Tavris, Carol. The bogus pipeline. Psychology Today, September,
    1974, pp. 85 ff. The interesting attitude measurement technique
    known as the bogus pipeline is discussed.

Keating, John P. A politician's guide to success on the stump: Hire
    a heckler. Psychology Today, April, 1971, pp. 70 ff. Does a
    speaker have a better chance of getting his message through to
    his audience when the audience is distracted? Several theories
    say "yes."

Etzioni, Amitai. Human beings are not very easy to change after all.
    Saturday Review, June 3, 1972. Cites the failure of warnings on
    smoking, etc., to develop the hypothesis that persuading people
    has little effect on their actual behavior.

CHAPTER 5

PREJUDICE AND DISCRIMINATION: WHY ALL TOO OFTEN

(AND WITH LITTLE REASON) DIFFERENCES COUNT

Objectives

[handwritten annotations: negative attitudes toward members of some distinct social group; preconceived notions about others which tend to persist; cognitive affective behavior]

1. Define prejudice and indicate how such cognitive factors as
    schemata and stereotypes relate to it. Also, list and define
    the components of attitudes and how these differ from discrim-
    ination. *[handwritten: is actions arising from prejudice attitudes]*

2. Describe how what others expect of us can shape our behavior.
    Emphasize the Skrypnek and Snyder (1982) study of males and
    females who were either informed correctly, incorrectly, or
    uninformed as to the sex of their partners in a "division of
    labor" game.

3. Illustrate subtle forms of discrimination by discussing the
    Gaertner-Dividio study of how the presence of bystanders
    influences helping of blacks by whites and the tokenism effect
    (Dutton and colleagues) as qualified by Rosenfeld and co-workers.

4. Describe how Brisham and colleagues' study (1982) of con-
    venience store clerks illustrated the tendencies by members of
    one group to see members of another group as similar in
    appearance. *[handwritten: Cross-group recognition]*

    [handwritten: list traits - identify social groups]

5. Indicate typical methods for measuring the components of pre-
    judice--stereotypes, feelings and discriminatory tendencies--
    and use the Moe and colleagues study (1982) to show how dis-
    criminatory behavior has changed over a decade and a half. *[handwritten: social distances scales]*

    [handwritten: attitude scales]

6. Using the story that began this chapter, indicate how conflict
    (for example, competition) among groups can lead to prejudice.
    How is conflict, including competition directly shown to in-
    fluence the development of prejudice (use the results of the
    famous "summer-camp" studies by Sherif and colleagues)?

7. Consider the "us vs. them" factor in prejudice by examining Tafjef and colleagues theory of why people boost the ingroup and depreciate the outgroup.

8. Entertain the tendency for people to see members of outgroups as "all acting the same" (behaviorally homogeneous) by attention to Park and Rothbart (1982) study of perceived stereotype endorsement by the opposite sex and sororities members' perceptions of women belonging to rival sororities.

9. Describe what a person with an "authoritarian personality" is like and how they got that way (how they were reared).

harsh punitive child-rearing practices

one who shows a pattern of submissive obedience to authority

10. Describe social learning processes and tell how the mass media contributes to social learning processes that promote prejudice.

attitudes are learned through exposure to views of others

11. Who are the major teachers of prejudice and how might their lessons be changed? In answering the question explore the Iowa-eye-color study? *parents*

12. Indicate why contact among members of different groups may reduce intergroup prejudice, and consider the conditions that must exist if contact is to have positive effects. Also, how does the "jigsaw method" act to reduce prejudice?

better acquainted, more equal, disconfirmation of stereotypes overcome illusion of out group homogeneity

13. What is the world's largest group to be the object of prejudice? Is the outlook getting better for that group? *yes*

women

14. Evaluate the characteristics, jobs and other pursuits that are typically assigned to females and those assigned to males.

submissive, dependent, gentle, passive, emotional   *assertiveness, decisiveness, leadership, self-assurance*

15. Assess the accuracy of stereotypes about females and males by reference to the study of business students (Steinberg and Shapiro, 1982) and the study of teachers' and parents' perceptions of boys' and girls' behavior (Lott, 1978).

16. How has women's contribution to the world of work changed in recent years and what is the current status of women "on the job?"

17. If men succeed on the job, with what are they attributed? Consider the same question as applied to women.

18. How do women compare to men in the way they behave as managers? Illustrate how the competency of women is undermined "on the job" by reference to the study of "card sorting" (Sanders and Schmidt, 1980).

19. Discuss the controversy surrounding "fear of success" in women and consider how "internal barriers" (Terborg, 1977) may actually inhibit the success of women "on the job."

20. Define sex role development (sex typing) and tell how the social learning notions of modeling and reinforcement shape the behavior of girls and boys.

58

21. Describe Bem's gender schemata theory, its influence on self-esteem, evidence in support of the point of view and Crane and Markus' (1982) rival "self-schemata" theory.

22. How did Markus and colleagues (1982) support their theory in their "me-not me" study?

23. What is "androgyny," how prevalent is it, and what controversy surrounds it?

24. "Conservatives" helped to kill ERA, but the authors assert that ERA supporters also contributed to the demise of the amendment. Discuss the three possible ways that supporters might have undermined their own cause.
1) Overly passionate appeals
2) spokeswomen who were unappealing
3) invoked reactance by threats

Who Done It?

Credit each of the concepts, theories, critical studies or important ideas listed below to the person or persons associated with each (e.g., item: Id-Ego-Superego; associated person: Freud). The correct answers are on the next page.

1. "gender schema theory" S. Bem

2. "self-schemata theory" Crane & Markus

3. famous eye color demonstration Jane Elliot

4. the first and most famous of the summer camp studies M. Sherif

5. the study of Florida convenience store clerks J. Brigham

6. "internal barriers" to success for women Terborg

7. the card sorting study Sanders & Schmidt

Define

Each of the critical concepts listed below have been defined in your textbook. For each provide the definition. Answers are on the next page.

1. Social learning theory — children pick the parent of the same sex and use them as a role model and receive rewards for imitating their behavior

2. Stereotype — beliefs and expectations held by individuals about the members of a particular group.

3. Adrogyny — the tendency to have the characteristics of both sexes

4. Tokenism *the tendency to act positively to objects of prejudice when it envolves little effort*

5. Authoritarianism *submissive obedience to authority harsh, punitive child-rearing practices*

Who Done It Answers

1. S. Bem (199)
2. Crane and Markus (201)
3. Jane Elliot (189)
4. M. Sherif and colleagues (182)
5. J. Brigham and colleagues (178)
6. Terborg (198)
7. Sanders and Schmidt (197)

Definitions

1. Children pick out the most similar parent (i.e., the parent of the same biological sex) for a model and receive rewards for imitating the behavior of that parent (185)

2. Beliefs and expectations held by individuals about the members of a particular group (171)

3. The tendency to have characteristics of both sexes (203)

4. The tendency to act in a positive, friendly manner toward objects of prejudice when the effort involved in the act is minimal (176)

5. involves submissive obedience to authority, and harsh, punitive child-rearing practices (185)

Matching

Match each concept on the left with an identifying phrase, word or sentence on the right. The answers are on the next page.

A. rival to "gender schema theory"
B. woman who succeeds at a "man's" job
C. source of a woman holding herself back
D. refers to boosting the ingroup and depreciating the outgroup
E. most important persons for determining prejudice in children
F. "submissive"
G. attitude and behavior
H. measures closeness with which other people are accepted in social relations
I. study showing how expectations of of others can shape our behavior

H 1. social distance
E 2. parents
I 3. "division of labor"
F 4. stereotype of women
B 5. lucky
G 6. prejudice and discrimination
C 7. "internal barriers"
A 8. "self-schemata theory"
D 9. "us vs. them"

60

Matching Answers

1. H 180
2. E 188
3. I 174
4. F 192
5. B 196
6. G 170
7. C 198
8. A 201
9. D 183

Is Something Wrong Here?

For each statement below indicate what is incorrect about the statement if anything. If there _is_ something wrong, answer "yes" and indicate what's wrong. If nothing is wrong, answer "no; this one is correct." At the end of this exercise you will find the answers.

wrong 1. Moe and colleagues investigated the willingness of white children to engage in close contact with black children. They found that children in ~~1979~~ 1966 showed less willingness than in 1966 1979.

wrong 2. "Eye of the storm" refers to a famous classroom demonstration in which some students ~~wore~~ had dark ~~contact lens~~ eyes and some students ~~wore~~ had light ~~lens~~ eyes and the latter discriminated against the former.

correct 3. The "jigsaw method" involves having elementary students each be responsible for part of a total assignment for their group.

wrong 4. In terms of stereotypes, women are seen as more dependent than men and men are seen as ~~less~~ more ambitious than women.

correct 5. "Fear of success" is the tendency to fear not being a success.

wrong 6. One reasonable solution to preventing the development of prejudice is to call parental attention to the influence of their ~~children~~'s attitudes and behaviors on attitudes and behaviors of ~~parents~~. _then children_

Is Something Wrong Here Answers

1. Yes; there was greater willingness in '79 than in '66. (180)

2. Close; naturally dark-eyed and naturally light-eyed children took turns being objects of discrimination (189)

3. No; this one is correct. (191)

4. Close again; the first part is correct, but men are seen as more ambitious than women (192)

5. Yes; "fear of success" is fear that one will be successful (198)

61

6. Yes; cause and effect are backwards. It is parents who
   influence children. (188)

True-False

Indicate whether each of the following statements is true or
false. Correct answers are at the end of this exercise.

F 1. "Prejudice" and "discrimination" are just different words for
   the same thing.

T 2. The basic components of an attitude are cognitive, affective
   and behavioral.

T 3. Gaertner and Dovidio (1977) staged an accident involving a
   white or a black victim. They found that when the subject was
   with two other witnesses of the accident, she was more likely
   to help the white than the black victim.

F 4. Park and Rothbart (1982) found that males and females saw their
   own sex as more homogeneous than the opposite sex.

T 5. The "social learning" point of view includes the notion that
   children may be directly rewarded for expressing prejudice.

T 6. Social Distance refers to the degree of closeness or intimacy
   to which individuals are willing to admit members of various
   social groups.

F 7. Contact between ingroup and outgroup members inevitable leads
   to a decrease in prejudice.

F 8. Authoritarianism research illustrates the ~~social cognition~~ *personality*
   approach to studying prejudice.

True-False Answers

1. False; "prejudice" refers to "attitude" and "discrimination"
   to behavior. (170)

2. True   (171)

3. True   (173)

4. False; they saw the opposite sex as more homogeneous. (186)

5. True   (185)

6. True   (185)

7. False; the contact must be cooperative, informal, and equal status if it is to lead to decreases in prejudice. (190)

8. False; it illustrates the personality approach. (185)

Fill in the Blanks

Complete the following statements by filling in the blanks with correct information. The answers are at the end of this exercise.

1. In the Sanders and Schmidt (1980) study that involved card sorting, female subjects sorted ___*more*___ cards if they thought they were working for a male _____ student.

2. According to the text, the ___*IEA*___ was defeated because radical women generated ___*reactance*___ when they threatened boycotts and disruptive activities.

3. Steinberg and Shapiro (1983) compared the personality traits of male and female ___*business*___ students and found few ___*sex*___ differences. ___*Female*___ students actually scored higher on toughmindedness.

4. The world's largest group to be objects of prejudice is ___*women*___. Their lot has gotten ___*better*___ in the last decade, but the effect seems to be leveling off.

5. Rosenfeld and colleagues (1982) exposed subjects to a ___*black*___ panhandler or a black ___*graduate*___ student seeking ___*research*___ funds and then later asked them to engage in ___*pro-minority*___ activities.

6. Sex-typing is the process by which children learn sexual ___*identity*___ and knowledge of behaviors and ___*traits*___ assumed by their culture to constitute ___*masculinity*___ and ___*femininity*___.

7. The possession of both masculine and feminine traits is called

_____*androgyny*_____.

Fill-in-the-Blank Answers

1. more; engineering (198)
2. Equal Rights Amendment (or ERA); reactance (204)
3. business; sex; female (193)
4. women; better (191)
5. black; graduate; research; prominiority ("civil rights" is
    acceptable) (176)
6. identity; traits; masculinity; femininity (last two in either
    order) (199)
7. androgyny (203)

d 1. In the study by Skrypnek and Snyder (1982) where males and females worked in pairs
   a. masculine tasks were available to subjects
   b. feminine tasks were available to subjects
   c. neutral tasks were available to subjects
   d. all of the above

d 2. Subtle forms of discrimination on the part of prejudiced persons include
   a. refusal to speak to persons who are the objects of prejudice
   b. withholding aid from objects of prejudice who need it
   c. the directing of trivial, tokenistic actions toward objects of prejudice
   d. both b and c

b 3. A stereotype is
   a. a type of stereo used mainly by minority persons
   b. beliefs and expectations about members of a particular group
   c. a pattern of behavior shown by bigoted people who are also members of a minority group
   d. a rare form of discrimination

b 4. If redheads are expected to be hotheads
   a. they may react the opposite of the expectation
   b. they may act according to expectations
   c. they may be careful not to confirm the expectation
   d. they may act in an inconsistent manner so as to confuse those who have expectations concerning them

d 5. Difficulty in recognizing members of another race
   a. would seem to have no practical consequences
   b. may influence the accuracy of eye-witness testimony
   c. may be interpreted by members of another race as an intentional slight or affront
   d. both b and c

d 6. In the "convenience store" study by Brigham and colleagues (1982)
   a. clerks showed about a 90% rate of correctly identifying an accomplice who had earlier made a purchase
   b. cross-race identification by whites was more accurate than by blacks
   c. clerks with more cross-race contact were poorer at cross-race identification
   d. clerks of both races were more successful at identifying members of their own race, relative to members of the other race

d 7. In the famous "summer camp" study by Sherif and colleagues
   a. interactions between groups were initially cordial
   b. boxing matches forced on the boys by the experimenters
      generated antagonism between groups
   c. conflict between groups was resolved by events which
      necessitated cooperative action by the groups
   d. both a and c

c 8. According to the story that began this chapter, some people think
   that
   a. Cubans are mainly highly educated
   b. Cubans tend to be upwardly mobile (striving to improve their
      social status)
   c. Cubans all behave in much the same way
   d. Cubans tend to be religious fanatics

a 9. Authoritarianism includes
   a. submissive obedience to authority
   b. a strong tendency to defy authority
   c. the use of as many categories to classify people
   d. a tendency to be unconventional

d 10. In the famous Eye of the Storm elementary school classroom demon-
    stration it was shown that
    a. the "goodness" (or lack of it) attributed to a group of people
       is "in the eye of the beholder"
    b. black children were singled out for antagonistic treatment
       because of their dark eye color
    c. dark-eyed children, regardless of their race, were the objects
       of prejudice in the classroom
    d. first dark-, and then light-eyed children were singled out
       and treated like real-life objects of prejudice

b 11. What currently controversial employment policy may actually
    reduce prejudice?
    a. equal security for management and employees
    b. affirmative action
    c. equal opportunity for people regardless of educational level
    d. no-fault contract

d 12. Which of the following are listed in the text as "stereotypic
    beliefs about men"?
    a. dominant   c. decisive
    b. ambitious   d. all of the above

a 13. How has the role of women in the work force changed from the
    early 70s to the early 80s?
    a. women now participate in work that was previously prohibited
       them
    b. women now are actually making much more relative to men than
       was the case in the early 70s
    c. women are now constituting almost half of the workers in the
       heavy construction industry
    d. women now constitute a smaller proportion of the total work
       force than was the case in the early 70s

a 14. Sanders and Schmidt (1980) had male and female subjects do a card-sorting task. What were the results of the study?
   a. both male and female subjects did better for the male "engineering student"
   b. only female subjects did better for the male "engineering student"
   c. only male subjects did better for the male "engineering student"
   d. male subjects showed less sexual bias than did female subjects

b 15. Sex-typing is
   a. a process by which children gain the identity and knowledge of behaviors and traits that are appropriate for their biological sex
   b. a process by which children gain the identity and knowledge of behaviors and traits that are assumed by their culture to constitute masculinity or femininity
   c. an inability to determine the appropriate role assigned to one's biological sex
   d. an ability to determine the appropriate behaviors expected of the opposite sex

Multiple Choice Answers

1. d 174	9. a 185
2. d 172	10. d 189
3. b 172	11. b 191
4. b 174	12. d 192
5. d 177	13. a 194
6. d 178	14. a 198
7. d 182	15. b 199
8. c 186	

Just for Fun: Some Additional Readings

U.S. News and World Report, Aug. 23, 1976, p. 50 (also see the article
    beginning on page 51). Are unattractive people objects of dis-
    crimination? Yes! according to this article.

Schuman, H. Are whites really more liberal?: Blacks aren't impressed.
    Psychology Today, Sept., 1974. Whites were becoming less pre-
    judiced in 1974, and the trend continues into the present (News-
    week, Feb. 26, 1979). But is it real change, does it signal an
    end to racism, do blacks buy it? This article attempts to answer
    those questions.

Parlee, M. The sexes under scrutiny: From old biases to new theories.
    Psychology Today, Nov., 1978. So you think that the sexes are dif-
    ferent. Well, males and females do differ in some ways, but
    maybe not in the ways you and others would expect them to differ.

Schwartz, J. She learned what it's like to be an old person in
    America. Peoria Journal Star, Jan., 21, 1983, A10. Someday all
    of us lucky enough to live long enough get to be members of a
    persecuted minority--elderly people. Want to know what it's like?
    Pat Moore, an attractive 28-year-old woman dressed up regularly
    as an elderly person. You may be frightened by what she exper-
    ienced.

Blount, R., Today's new klan. Parade, Aug. 30, 1981. A self-pro-
    claimed Southern "redneck" infiltrated the Klan and was shocked
    by what he discovered. You will be too.

Snyder, M. Self-fulfilling stereotypes. Psychology Today, July, 1982.
    If you would be pleased to find some group of people "stupid,
    lazy, dirty, etc.," they may be happy to accommodate you.

CHAPTER 6

ATTRACTION, FRIENDSHIP, AND LOVE

Objectives

1. Describe our emotional evaluation of and our behavior toward
    persons at various levels of the interpersonal attraction
    dimension.

2. Discuss the relationship between propinquity and interpersonal
    attraction.

3. Discuss the impact of repeated exposure to a person on our
    attitudes toward him/her.

4. Discuss how attraction is affected by the feelings induced by
    music and news content.

5. Summarize the reinforcement-affect model of attraction.

6. Discuss the research on affiliation behavior.
    a) Describe the differences between persons high vs. low in
        need for affiliation.
    b) How do fear and embarrassment affect peoples' desire to
        affiliate?

7. Describe how appearance, especially physical attractiveness,
    influences attraction.

8. Explain how matching affects romantic choices.

9. Summarize the effect that each of the following has on ratings
    of attractiveness:
    a) Body features
    b) Facial features
    c) The contrast effect
    d) "Closing time"

10. What is the effect of attitude similarity on liking?
    a) How does social comparison explain the similarity effect?
    b) How does balance theory explain it?

11. Summarize the effects of personality/behavioral similarity on liking.

12. Compare the impact of need compatibility and need complementarity on liking.

13. Discuss the exceptions to the similarity-attraction effect found in the Focus on Research box.

14. How does level of self-disclosure relate to liking?

15. How do we evaluate others who make positive or negative evaluations of us?

16. How is our attraction influenced by whether the other person helps vs. doesn't help?

17. What three factors seem to be necessary for a person to experience passionate love?

18. Compare passionate love and companionate love.

19. Discuss peoples' responses to rejection.

20. What factors determine whether a relationship will last?

Who Done It?

Credit each of the concepts, theories, critical studies or important ideas listed below to the person or persons associated with each (e.g., item: Id-Ego-Superego; associated person: Freud). Answers are on the next page.

1. study showing that repeated exposure leads to attraction
   Moreland & Zajonc

2. study showing that the presence of liked music increases attraction to stranger
   May & Hamilton

3. study showing that attractive individuals spend more time gazing at themselves in a mirror
   McDonald & Eilenfield

4. study showing that potential partners are perceived to be more attractive at closing time
   Pennebaker et al.

5. study showing that attraction for a stranger depends on the proportion of similar attitudes expressed by that person
   Byrne & Nelson

6. Study showing that self-disclosing males are generally rated more negatively than self-disclosing females, although it depends on the topic

   Kleinke & Kahn

7. study showing that both extreme dissimilarity and extreme similarity are aversive, as predicted by uniqueness theory

   Snyder & Endelman

Who Done It Answers

1. Moreland and Zajonc (215)
2. May and Hamilton (216)
3. McDonald and Eilenfield (223)
4. Pennebaker et al. (225)
5. Byrne and Nelson (227)
6. Kleinke and Kahn (232)
7. Snyder and Endelman (231)

Define

Each of the critical concepts listed below have been defined in your textbook. For each provide the definition. Answers are on the next page.

1. interpersonal attraction : *the positive/negative dimension along which we evaluate others*
2. propinquity : *the physical distance between people which is determined by environmental factors*
3. need for affiliation : *the desire of people to be with others*
4. reinforcement-affect model : *the theory which says that our likes/dislikes of others is determined by how we happen to feel when we encounter them*
5. balance theory : *the theory which says that people expect to be in agreement with those they like*
6. self-disclosure : *the exchanging of information about oneself and one's feeling usually as a part of friendship formation*
7. need compatability hypothesis : *states that having similar needs is the basis of interpersonal attraction*
8. need complementarity hypothesis : *states that having opposite reinforcing traits is the basis for attraction*
9. companionate love : *the mature and lasting love that sometimes develops out of passionate love*

Definitions

1. positive-negative dimension along which we evaluate other people (212)

2. physical distance between people as determined by environmental factors (213)

3. the desire of people to be with others (219)

4. the theory which says that our likes/dislikes of other people are determined by how we happen to feel when we encounter them; if some stimulus in our environment is making us feel good, this good feeling becomes associated with the encountered person (218)

5. the theory which says that people expect to be in agreement with those they like; people prefer this type of arrangement because it is more symmetrical (228)

6. the exchanging with a partner of information about oneself and one's feelings; usually accompanies friendship formation (229)

7. states that having similar needs is the basis of interpersonal attraction (229)

8. states that having mutually reinforcing traits that are opposites is the basis for attraction (229)

9. the mature and lasting love that sometimes develops out of passionate love (237)

Matching

Match each concept or idea on the left with an identifying phrase, word or sentence on the right. Answers are on the next page.

A. being ignored
B. uniqueness theory
C. social comparison
D. bearer of offspring
E. attraction
F. love/hate
G. jealousy
H. powerful provider

_D_ 1. what males seek in partner (according to sociobiologists)

_H_ 2. what females seek in partner (according to sociobiologists)

_A_ 3. cue for disliking

_E_ 4. poles for attraction dimension

_G_ 5. rival causes this

_B_ 6. postulates motive to be different

_C_ 7. mechanism behind fear-induced affiliation

_E_ 8. our evaluation of another person

72

Matching Answers

1. D	(225)	5. G	(238)
2. H	(225)	6. B	(230)
3. A	(233)	7. C	(221)
4. F	(212)	8. E	(212)

Is Something Wrong Here?

For each statement below indicate what is wrong about the statement, if anything. If there _is_ something wrong, answer "yes" and
indicate what's wrong. If nothing is wrong, answer "No; this one is
correct." At the end of this exercise you will find the answers.

wrong
1. Repeated exposure to a stimulus generally has the effect of
    decreasing our liking for the stimulus. *increasing*

correct
2. In the classic Schachter (1959) studies, subjects expecting to
    receive painful electric shocks preferred waiting with other
    subjects rather than waiting alone.

wrong
3. Subjects expecting to take part in an embarrassing experiment
    preferred waiting for the experiment with other subjects rather
    than waiting alone.

wrong
4. The mechanism operating to produce increased affiliation in
    response to fear seems to be higher-order conditioning. *social conditioning*

wrong
5. When asked to rate their level of attraction for males of
    various heights, women indicate a preference for tall males. *median height*

wrong
6. The text explains the fact that the perceived attractiveness of
    bar patrons changes as closing time approaches in terms of the
    perceivers' drunkenness. *need*

wrong
7. While traditionally sex-typed males show a high level of
    responsiveness to the physical attractiveness of a partner,
    traditionally sex-typed females do not. *Both male & female do*

wrong
8. Attractive members of both sexes are more assertive than less
    attractive persons. *males are, females aren't (less attractive females are more assertive*

wrong
9. Studies have documented no behavioral differences between
    attractive and unattractive persons.

wrong
10. Because their relationship is based on friendship, dating *more*
    couples who are mismatched for physical attractiveness are less
    likely to break-up than well-matched couples.

correct
11. The similarity/attraction hypothesis is more firmly accepted
    for the effects of attitude similarity than for personality/
    behavioral similarity.

12. Dominant persons like others who are dominant, whereas sub-missive persons like others who are submissive.

13. People share more intimate self-disclosures when talking to a single friend than they do in groups of three or more.

14. For every topic studied, females who are highly disclosing are rated more positively than males who are highly disclosing.

15. People like others who engage in self-disclosure that is considerably more intimate than they themselves are willing to engage in.

16. Persons high in sensation-seeking are attracted to others who are the opposite of themselves.

17. We like people who evaluate us positively even if the evaluation is inaccurate.

18. Emotional reactions such as being frightened or being angry can be mistakenly interpreted as "being in love."

19. The reaction on the part of most people when they are rejected by a potential partner is to try even harder to obtain the partner.

Is Something Wrong Here? Answers

1. Yes; repeated exposure generally increases our liking. (215)

2. No; this one is correct. (221)

3. Yes; when the experiment involved upcoming embarrassment, subjects wanted to wait alone. (221)

4. Yes; the mechanism seems to be social comparison. (221)

5. Yes; while tall males seem to be preferred as political candidates, males of medium height are preferred as dates. (224)

6. Yes; the reason is that perceivers' needs become greater as the evening progresses. (225)

7. Yes; traditionally sex-typed persons of both sexes show a high level of responsiveness to physical attractiveness. (222)

8. Yes; attractive males are more assertive, but for females it is less attractive individuals who are more assertive. (223)

9. Yes; question 8 referred to assertiveness differences, and there are also gazing differences, among others. (226)

10. Yes; mismatched couples more frequently break up. (226)

74

11. No; this one is correct. (228)

12. Yes; Palmer and Byrne (1970) found that relatively dominant persons are preferred, regardless of one's own orientation. (228)

13. No; this one is correct. (229)

14. Just a little something; highly disclosing females are generally rated more positively than highly disclosing males. However, when revealing feelings of competitiveness, there is no difference between the sexes. (232)

15. Yes; people like others who disclose about as much as they do. (232)

16. No; this one is correct. (230)

17. No; this one is correct. (233)

18. No; this one is correct. (236)

19. Yes; most people give up when rejected, which is why "playing hard to get" can backfire. (239)

True-False

Indicate whether each of the following statements is true or false. Correct answers are at the end of the exercise.

F 1. Repeated exposure leads to increased liking for a stranger even when the stranger gives the subject punishments.

F 2. Female subjects showed more liking for males shown in photos when they rated the photos while music was playing.

T 3. When a subject hears good news just before encountering a stranger, the stranger is liked more.

T 4. Males high in need for affiliation are self-confident, talk a lot to attractive females, and show satisfaction as an involving relationship progresses.

T 5. The lowest level of attraction was shown by college students to a stranger when the stranger evoked negative feelings and low concern.

T 6. Males who had been watching Charlie's Angels on television rated a female of average attractiveness lower than did males who had not been exposed to the glamorous angels.

T 7. A person who has attractive same-sex friends is given more positive ratings.

8. Having a desirable first name ("Jennifer") produces more positive ratings than having an undesirable first name ("Gertrude").

9. Physically attractive persons spend more time gazing at themselves as they walk past a mirrored wall than less attractive persons.

10. It is easier to remember having previously seen an attractive person as compared to a less attractive person.

11. Research has consistently found that pairs of friends and spouses are more similar in attitudes than randomly-matched pairs.

12. Experimental studies of the attitude similarity/attraction relationship fail to confirm a causal relationship.

13. Children no longer show any concern over the age of their play companions after age seven or eight.

14. Research has provided strong support for the need complementarity hypothesis as a basis for a successful marriage and little support for the need compatibility hypothesis.

15. One of the indications that a friendship is developing between two people is an increase in their tendency to engage in self-disclosure.

16. People generally like others who are similar to themselves in their characteristic level of self-disclosure.

17. Being ignored by others is a negative experience which leads us to dislike whoever it is that is ignoring us.

18. Passionate love is experienced in the same way in every culture.

True-False Answers

1. False; repeated exposure generally increases liking, but not when the stimulus person delivers punishment to the subjects. (215)

2. Almost true, but not quite. Music increased liking only when it was liked music. (216)

3. True   (217)

4. True   (219)

5. True   (222)

6. True   (225)

7. True (223)

8. True (223)

9. True (226)

10. False; it is actually easier to remember having seen the less
    attractive person. (226)

11. True (227)

12. False; the relationship has been strongly and consistently found.
    (227)

13. False; in fact, after age seven or eight there is an increasing
    tendency to seek companions close to their own age. (229)

14. False; need compatibility has strong support and need comple-
    mentarity has little. (229)

15. True (229)

16. True (232)

17. True (233)

18. False; in order to experience love, individuals must be ex-
    posed to cultural influences that define love. (236)

Fill-in-the-Blanks

    Complete the following statements by filling in the blanks with
correct information. The answers are at the end of the exercise.

1. The fact that friendships tend to develop between people who

    live near each other or work together demonstrates the effect

    of _*propinquity*_ on attraction.

2. When friendship development is affected by distance factors

    because these factors are related to the ease of interaction,

    this is _*functional propinquity*_.

3. The proposal that our evaluation of and attraction to others

    depends on the emotional response elicited in their presence

    by our surroundings is the central idea of _*reinforcement/affect*_

    theory.

4. The text argues that the process underlying the effects of propinquity on liking is _repeated exposure_.

5. The process underlying the reinforcement-affect model is _second-order classical conditioning_.

6. The personality dimension that is related to our need to have friends and to be with people is the _need for affiliation_.

7. The _matching_ hypothesis proposes that we choose a partner who is roughly equal to ourselves in physical attractiveness.

8. Where P and O like each other and they disagree about X, the relationship is _imbalanced_.

9. The hypothesis that we like others whose personality needs are similar to our own is the _need/compatibility_ hypothesis.

10. The hypothesis that mutually-reinforcing differences are the basis for attraction is the _need complementary_ hypothesis.

11. _Uniqueness_ theory proposes that people are often threatened by similarity, and notes that a person in a group where he is very similar to everyone else will often act in a way to stress his differentness and individuality.

12. The principle of _reciprocity_ states that we like people who like us.

13. Research has shown that we like those who evaluate us _positively_ and dislike those who evaluate us _negatively_.

14. The three major conditions necessary for a person to experience passionate love are: 1) _being raised in a culture that believes in love_ ; 2) _the presence of an appropriate love-object_ ; 3) _emotional arousal that is interpreted as love_.

15. A brain chemical associated with being in love is also found in _chocolate_.

16-19. Fill in the blanks with regard to differences between the sexes.

16. With regard to the level of self-disclosure between pairs of same-sex friends, pairs of _female_ friends engage in more intimate disclosure.

17. _Males_ are found to fall in love more easily; _females_ fall out of love more easily.

18. _Males_ report having been more often rejected by members of the opposite sex.

19. _Males_ have a higher level of dating anxiety.

20. The deep, genuine and lasting love relationship that sometimes grows out of passionate love is _compassionate_ love.

Fill-in-the-Blanks Answers

1. propinquity (214)
2. functional propinquity (214)
3. reinforcement-affect (218)
4. repeated exposure (218)
5. second-order classical conditioning (218)
6. need for affiliation (219)
7. matching (226)
8. imbalanced (228)
9. need-compatability (229)
10. need-complementarity (229)
11. Uniqueness (230)
12. reciprocity (233)
13. positively; negatively (233)

14. being raised in a culture that believes in love; presence of an appropriate love-object; emotional arousal that is interpreted as love. (235)
15. chocolates (236)
16. female (229)
17. males; females (237)
18. males (238)
19. males (238)
20. companionate (237)

Multiple Choice

1. Your text defines the term attraction to be our _____ another person.   *c*
   a. behavior toward
   b. beliefs about
   c. evaluation of
   d. impression of

2. Choose the location where propinquity has been shown to have no effect on friendship formation.   *d*
   a. in a big city housing project for the elderly
   b. in classroom seating arrangements
   c. in college dormitories
   d. none of the above (i.e., propinquity affects friendship development in all of the above)

3. Which has been found to increase attraction toward a stranger?   *e*
   a. viewing a happy movie
   b. hearing a broadcast reporting good news
   c. listening to music we enjoy
   d. a and c
   e. a, b, and c

4. You have just eaten a good meal, drunk a great wine, and had very satisfactory love-making. As a result, you are feeling M-E-L-L-O-W. Suddenly, out from under the bed comes a stranger. According to the reinforcement-affect model of attraction, how should you react?   *a*
   a. you should like this person, since you are in a good mood
   b. you should become angry, since this person poses an obvious threat to your current good mood
   c. you should react in a neutral manner, since your good mood neatly cancels the threat you feel
   d. the reinforcement-affect model makes no predictions in strange situations such as this one

5. Fish, et al. (1978) found that subjects expecting to take part in an embarrassing experiment preferred to wait_____; Schachter (1959) found that subjects expecting to take part in a fear-arousing experiment preferred to wait _____.   *c*
   a. alone; alone
   b. together; together
   c. alone; together
   d. together; alone

6. Sociobiologists explain the physical attractiveness preferences of men and women by suggesting that   *e*
   a. males are attracted by cues associated with bearing offspring
   b. females are attracted to cues associated with powerful providers
   c. in a given culture people learn to agree as to what is attractive
   d. standards of beauty fluctuate dramatically across time in a given culture
   e. both a and b

7. Physically attractive males are judged to be _____ than less attractive males.
   a. brighter
   b. better adjusted
   c. more masculine
   d. all of the above

8. In which sex are attractive members more assertive?
   a. males
   b. females
   c. both males and females
   d. neither males nor females

9. When dating couples are mismatched for physical attractiveness
   a. they are more likely to break up than well-matched couples
   b. their relationship tends to be stronger because it is based on friendship rather than sex
   c. the more attractive partner tends to worry more about the possible unfaithfulness of the less attractive partner
   d. both a and c
   e. a, b, and c

10. Suppose that during a conversation with one of your best friends, you discover that he/she dislikes social psychology and your professor. You, on the other hand, like both of these things very much. (After all, you are an individual of impeccable good taste!) Under these conditions, your relationship with your friend can be described as
    a. imbalanced
    b. nonbalanced
    c. balanced
    d. none of the above; it is your friend who is unbalanced

11. The _____ hypothesis states that persons with similar needs will like each other; the _____ hypothesis states that people will like others with mutually reinforcing compatible needs.
    a. need compatability; need complementarity
    b. reinforcement-affect; need complementarity
    c. need compatability; reinforcement-affect
    d. need complementarity; need compatability

12. On which topic of discussion is a female who is highly disclosing rated as negatively as a male who is highly disclosing?
    a. a parent's suicide
    b. their own sexual preferences
    c. feelings of competitiveness and a desire to be successful
    d. all of the above
    e. none of the above, i.e., highly disclosing females are rated more positively than highly disclosing males for all the topics

13. Uniqueness theory suggests that you may try to do something to stress your uniqueness when you are in a group in which you are very _____ every else; you may try to conform and blend into the mass when you are very _____ everyone else.
    a. similar to; different from
    b. different from; similar to
    c. similar to; similar to
    d. different from; different from

14. <u>Statement A</u>. We like people who evaluate us positively and dislike people who evaluate us negatively.
    <u>Statement B</u>. Being ignored by others causes a person to assume that people don't like him very much.
    a. both statements are true
    b. both statements are false
    c. statement A is true; statement B is false
    d. statement B is true; statement A is false

15. Which of the following is true?
    a. love is a universal experience, and marriages have always been based on love
    b. virtually no adults report having experienced "love at first sight"
    c. emotional arousal is not one of the necessary conditions for the experience of passionate love
    d. cultural influences teach us what love is

<u>Multiple Choice Answers</u>

1. c	(212)	9. a	(226)
2. d	(214)	10. a	(228)
3. e	(217)	11. a	(229)
4. a	(218)	12. c	(232)
5. c	(221)	13. a	(230)
6. e	(225)	14. a	(233)
7. d	(222)	15. d	(235)
8. a	(223)		

Just for Fun: Some Additional Readings

Peele, Stanton and Brodsky, Archie. Interpersonal heroin: Love can be an addiction. _Psychology Today_, August, 1974, pp. 22 ff. The authors argue that middle-class dependency on spouses and lovers is akin to dependency on drugs. Discusses addictive vs. mature love.

Berscheid, Ellen and Walster, Elaine. Beauty and the best. _Psychology Today_. March, 1972, pp. 42 ff. The way in which a variety of interpersonal behaviors are affected by the physical attractiveness of the participants is discussed.

Walster, Elaine, Piliavin, Jane, and Walster, G. Wm. The hard-to-get-woman. _Psychology Today_, September, 1973, pp. 80 ff. Developes the hypothesis that men like women who are hard for other men to get, but easy for them. Explanations for the phenomenon are presented.

Selman, R. and Selman, A. Children's ideas about friendship: A new theory. _Psychology Today_, October, 1979. "How do I like thee, let me count the ways." The number and complexity of the "ways" varies with the age of the child.

CHAPTER 7

SOCIAL INFLUENCE: CHANGING THE BEHAVIOR OF OTHERS

Objectives:

both spoken + unspoken rules about proper behavior

1. Define "conformity" and tell how it differs from "obedience" and "compliance." Also, indicate the meaning of social norms and how these relate to conformity. *Conformity is changing behavior to adhere to widely accepted norms / obedience is change due to direct command* *it social norms*

2. Thoroughly describe the Asch "lines" method of studying conformity, indicate the level of conformity generally obtained with this method and indicate the two types of social influence exerted in these types of experiments. *normative & informational* *75% at least once*

3. Describe how the problem of "inefficiency" that accompanies use of the Asch "lines" method is solved by use of the Crutchfield method. *An apparatus of lights replaces the confederates and mimics the effects of confederates by controlling what each participant's lead to believe are the answers of all other participants*

4. Define "reference groups" and indicate how attraction to them influences people. *groups that we like and with whom we compare ourselves. we become more like those that we are around a lot*

5. Discuss the relationship between the size of a group that exerts conformity pressures and the effect of that pressure. Also tell how Wilder (1977) has supported his contention that suspected "collusion" limits the relationship between group size and conformity level. *Most conformity is in groups of 3-5; conformity diminishes after that*

6. Indicate how having an "ally" can reduce conformity, regardless of the characteristics of the ally. Also consider the Stroebe and Diehl (1981) demonstration that having an ally can backfire when a person conforms despite presence of the ally. *Study where students were asked to write an essay supporting repayment of grants*

7. Describe the issues that surround the controversy concerning possible sex differences in conformity. In so doing, be able to answer the following question: "What are the factors that determine when sex differences in conformity are likely to be observed?" Also consider Eagly and Wood's (1982) notion that sex differences in conformtiy are in the "eye of the beholder." *When material used in testing are sex oriented. when male researchers are used. when individuals are exposed to social pressure to conform and are observed by all*

8. Consider why we often conform by discussing the determinants of conformity, "past reinforcement" and "social comparison." Provide examples of how both determinants operate. *we learn early that being like others is good* *human beings have a strong drive to evaluate their own opinions & abilities and need others to do that*

9. Contrast the explanations of how minorities exert influence offered by Holland ("idiosyncracy credits") and Moscovici ("consistent dissent") by attention to the study of Bray and colleagues (1982). *first conform then dissent.* *dissent from the start*

10. Define "ingratiation" and give three common direct methods of implementing the technique of influence as well as suggest more subtle methods of ingratiation. *technique for obtaining compliance based on request first increasing the attractiveness* *shared opinion* *excellent task performance* *flattery*

11. Describe the foot-in-the-door technique of influence, its generality, Freedman and Fraser's (1966) study of the phenomenon and Rittle's (1981) attempt to decide between rival explanations of why the method works.

12. Describe the door-in-the-face technique of influence, the demonstration of the phenomenon by Cialdini and colleagues (1975), the two rival explanations of the method as well as when it works and when it doesn't, relative to the foot-in-the-door technique.

13. Describe the "everyday" use of "lowballing," as well as the experimental demonstration of the phenomenon by Cialdini and colleagues (1978). Then consider the Burger and Petty (1981) attempt to decide between the "commitment" and "unfulfilled obligation" explanations of the phenomenon.

14. Thoroughly describe the standard obedience experiment by Milgram and its results. Also consider the experiments by Milgram dealing with factors influencing level of influence. What happens when the standard experiment is repeated in other countries?

15. List and describe the factors that determine whether people will obey, with special attention to the "graduation" suggestion by Gilbert (1981). Then consider the three ways to lower the likelihood of destructive obedience.

16. Define Bandura's notion of "modeling" and tell how "social models" can be used to generate desirable change by reference to the study by Jekibchuk and Smeriglio (1976).

Who Done It?

Credit each of the concepts, theories, critical studies or important ideas listed below to the person or persons associated with each (e.g., item: Id-Ego-Superego; associated person: Freud). The correct answers are on the next page.

1. obedience to authority   *Milgram*

2. standard and comparison lines   *Asch*

3. booths or isolation compartments for studying conformity.   *Crutchfield*

4. studied sex relevance of conformity items   *Sistrunk & McDavid*

5. reviewed literature on conformity and suggested that females may not conform more than males   *Eagly*

6. leader of the research team that investigated both "door-in-the-face" and "low-balling"   *Cialdini*

7. supported his conclusion that "collusion" limits the relationship between group size and conformity   *Wilder*

8. the theorist who suggested that "graduation" may partially account for the results of Milgram's studies   *Gilbert*

Define

Each of the critical concepts listed below have been defined in your textbook. For each provide the definition. Answers are on the next page.

1. conformity — *changing behavior to adhere to widely accepted beliefs or standards*

2. compliance — *changing behavior or response to direct requests from others*

3. obedience — *changing behavior in response to direct commands of others particularly when they have means of enforcing the command*

4. social influence — *any action performed by one or more persons meant to change the attitudes, behavior or feelings of one or more persons*

5. social norm — *the spoken and unspoken rules about how we should behave*

6. normative social influence — *involves our tendency to conform to the positive expectations of others*

7. informational social influence — *involves our tendency to employ others as the source of authoritative information*

8. reference group — *a group that we like and are like to whom we compare ourselves*

9. social reinforcement — *the praise or reward that comes from conforming*

10. social comparison — *checking one's own opinions against the opinions of others who are similar to us*

87

11. idiosyncrasy credits — *those credits, that a dissenting member of a group gets toward conformity, which can later be cashed in to exert influence on the views of others.*

12. consistent dissent — *stating opposition to the majority from the beginning and sticking with it.*

13. reciprocal consessions — *the explanation for the door in the face process when a requester backs down from the initial big request, then the requestee feels compelled to grant the smaller request.*

Who Done It Answers

1. Milgram (274)
2. Asch (250)
3. Crutchfield (252)
4. Sistrunk and McDavid (258)
5. Eagly (258)
6. Cialdini (269-72)
7. Wilder (254)
8. Gilbert (277)

Definitions

1. changing behaviors to adhere to widely accepted beliefs or standards (248)

2. changing behavior in response to direct requests from others (248)

3. changing behavior in response to direct commands of others (249)

4. any actions performed by one or more persons to change the attitudes, behavior, or feelings of one or more others (248)

5. spoken and unspoken rules concerning how we ought to behave (249)

6. involves our tendency to conform to the positive expectations of others (250

7. involves our tendency to employ other persons as a source of information (251)

8. a group that we like; to whom we compare ourselves (253)

9. the praise or material reward that comes with conforming (260)

10. checking one's one opinions against those of people who are similar to oneself is part of the process of "social comparisons" (260)

11. credits due to conformity on the part of group members holding dissenting views (262)

12. stating opposition to the majority from the beginning and sticking with dissension. (262)

13. in door-in-the-face process, requester backs down from initial large request and makes requestee feel the need to reciprocate the consession (269)

Matching

Match each concept on the left with an identifying phrase, word or sentence on the right. The answers are on the next page.

A. door-in-the-face
B. foot-in-the-door
C. conformity research
D. ingratiation
E. modeling effects
F. act of conformity
G. rival explanations of foot-in-the-door
H. used to treat social isolation
I. a 1981 explanation of Milgram's studies

D 1. flattery
B 2. small request, then big request
E 3. changing behavior as a result of observing the behaviors of others
G 4. self-perceptions vs. positive feelings about help situations
I 5. "graduation"
A 6. big request, then small request
F 7. going along with society's expectations about how we should behave
C 8. standard and comparison lines
H 9. social models

Is Something Wrong Here?

For each statement below indicate what is incorrect about the statement if anything. If there _is_ something wrong, answer "yes" and indicate what's wrong. If nothing is wrong, answer "no; this one is correct." Answers are on the next page.

wrong
1. Recent research (Stroebe and Diehl, 1981) indicates a failure to replicate earlier results supposedly showing that the "ally" effect can backfire.

wrong
2. When a person has one lone ally in a group that otherwise is 100% against her point of view, conformity increases.

wrong
3. Compared to the Asch "lines" method, the Crutchfield method of studying conformity is highly inefficient.

correct
4. When there is direct surveillance of subjects by others, women may conform more than men.

correct
5. "Ingratiation" is being nice to someone in order to get something from her/him.

wrong
6. The most common form of ingratiation is buying~~ someone an~~ expensive gift. _flattery_

correct
7. "Unfulfilled obligation" is an explanation of "low balling."

89

        1. D 264   6. A 268
        2. B 265   7. F 248
        3. E 278   8. C 251
        4. G 266-7   9. H 278
        5. I 277

Is Something Wrong Here Answers

1. Yes, it's the other way around; Stroebe and Diehl (1981) confirm the "backfire effect." (256)

2. Yes; it decreases significantly. (254)

3. Yes; again, it's the other way around; the Crutchfield method is more efficient. (252)

4. No; this one is correct. (258)

5. No; this one is correct. (264)

6. Yes. Are you kidding!; flattery is much cheaper. (264)

7. No; this one is correct. (273)

True-False

Indicate whether each of the following statements is true or false. Correct answers are at the end of this exercise.

1. Unlike the "foot-in-the-door" technique, the "door-in-the-face" technique seems to work only when a different person makes both requests and when there is a long time interval between requests.

2. A reference group is one about which we make negative references.

3. Destructive obedience can be countered if there are available persons whose actions show that obedience is inappropriate.

4. "Social comparison" involves comparing the customs of different socieites.

5. The Milgram experiments have been performed only in America.

6. "Self-presentation" is a process that can be used to explain the "door-in-the-face" method of influence.

7. Methods of ingratiation are all transparent and obvious.

8. "Commitment" is a process that provides an explanation of the "foot-in-the-door" method.

True-False Answers

1. False; "door-in-the-face" seems to work only when the same person makes both requests and when there is a short interval between requests. (270)

2. Not so; we are attracted to it and make positive references to it. (253)

3. True. (280)

4. Wrong; social comparison refers to comparing ourselves with persons whose circumstances are similar to our own. (260)

5. False; these experiments have also been performed in several other countries. (276)

6. True. (269)

7. False; some such methods are quite subtle. (264)

8. False; commitment can be used to explain "low-balling." (272)

Fill in the Blanks

Complete the following statements by filling in the blanks with correction information. The answers are at the end of this exercise.

1. The basic procedure involved in _low-balling_ is to get a person to make a decision and then shift the basis for the decision.

2. _low-balling_ may work because, once a person has made a decision, he/she would look like a "hasty" decision maker if he/she backed out and also he/she would waste all the effort it took to make the decision.

3. The "cover story" presented to subjects in Milgram's obedience experiments so that they would not be suspicious was that they would be participating in a _learning_ experiment.

4. Not only men, but also ___*women*___ and ___*children*___ have performed in the Milgram experiments.

5. Subjects in the Milgram experiments were more likely to disobey if they were made to feel ___*responsible*___ for any harm coming to the "learner" and if they had been presented with a person to act as a ___*model*___ of disobedience.

6. ___*"Unfulfilled obligation"*___ is a new explanation of low balling and the commitment explanation.

7. According to Eagly and Wood (1982) sex differences in conformity may be in the ___*eye of the beholder*___.

8. If women are under direct ___*surveillance*___, they may conform more than men.

Fill-in-the-Blank Answers

1. "low balling" (272)
2. "Low balling" (272)
3. learning   (274)
4. women and children (276)
5. responsible, model (276)
6. "Unfulfilled obligation"   (272)
7. the eye of the beholder   (258)
8. surveillance   (258)

d 1. Conformity is
   a. changing behavior in response to direct commands from others
   b. changing behavior in response to direct requests from others
   c. changing behavior as a result of simple observation of the behaviors of others
   d. changing behaviors to adhere to widely accepted beliefs or standards

a 2. Which of the following norms are helpful rather than hinderances?
   a. "You're not supposed to cut in line."
   b. "Men should wear suit and tie, women dresses."
   c. "You should be careful what you say around strangers."
   d. "Be careful not to stand out in a crowd."

d 3. Which of the following are among Deutsch and Gerard's components of social influence?
   a. normative   c. informational
   b. retributional   d. both a and c

a 4. A reference group is
   a. a group that we like; to whom we compare ourselves
   b. an irrelevant group for a given person
   c. simply an important group regardless of for whom it is important
   d. any of the large groups that we are all aware of

c 5. Wilder (1977) supported his theory of the relationship between group size and conformity by
   a. showing that the bigger the group, the greater the conformity obtained
   b. showing that the bigger the group the less the conformity obtained
   c. showing that more conformity is obtained by pressure from two independent groups of two each than from one group of four
   d. showing that group size has nothing to do with conformity

d 6. In the study by Stroebe and Diehl (1981) cognitive dissonance in a conformity experiment
   a. subjects were asked to write an essay against their point of view
   b. some of them heard an accomplice refuse to write a counter-attitudinal essay
   c. some of them heard an accomplice agree to write a counter-attitudinal essay
   d. all of the above

c 7. One circumstance in which females might conform more than males is
   a. when the experimenter is female
   b. when the task is more familiar to females
   c. when others exercise direct surveillance over subjects
   d. when subjects perform in private

93

C 8. Concerning minorities
   a. they are always the influencees rather than the influencers
   b. they have little influence by definition
   c. under certain circumstances, they may have considerable
      influence on majorities
   d. both a and b

d 9. In the study by Bray and colleagues (1982)
   a. "idiosyncrasy credits" was supported equally strongly for
      males and females
   b. neither the "idiosyncrasy credits" nor the "consistent
      dissent" theories received support
   c. only the "idiosyncrasy credits" point of view received any
      support
   d. "idiosyncrasy credits" and "consistent dissent" were equally
      supported by results for female subjects

C 10. When Freedman and Frazer (1966) called some people on the phone
    to ask them some simple questions about a soap product and then
    later asked them to allow a crew to come search their house
    a. no recipient of the first call granted the search request
    b. all recipients of the first call granted the search request
    c. more recipients of the first call granted the search request
       than comparison persons who received only the search request
    d. fewer people complied with the search request than was the
       case for persons who received the search request first and
       the soap questions second

d 11. The "foot-in-the-door" technique is most likely to fail when
    a. the large request is very costly
    b. the large request involves unpleasant behaviors
    c. the first request makes the person who complies with it feel
       like "the kind of person who offers help to people who re-
       quest it"
    d. both a and b

d 12. Which of the following are explanations of the "door-in-the-
    face" technique?
    a. self-perception   c. commitment
    b. unfulfilled obligation   d. reciprocal concessions

a 13. According to the "commitment" explanation of low balling
    a. a person becomes cognitively committed to granting a request
       and finds it hard to back down, even when the initial request
       is altered
    b. after granting a request, a person becomes committed to
       granting no further request
    c. before becoming committed to an initial request, the target
       of a request carefully examines that which he is being asked
       to grant
    d. after becoming committed to both of two requests, the target
       of requests is likely to grant any number of requests in the
       future

14. Which of the following were among the procedures used by
    Milgram to study obedience?
    a. actual shocks were delivered to a "learner" when he made
       errors on a "learning task"
    b. shocks indicated on a shock panel manipulated by subjects
       indicated voltages up to 450
    c. subjects could clearly see the "learner" suffering from the
       shocks that he/she delivered
    d. all of the above

15. Why does obedience occur in the Milgram's experiment?
    a. people are inherently submissive
    b. subjects are assumed to be responsible for outcomes in the
       situation in which they operate
    c. in effect, the experimenter starts with a small request
       and then follows it with a large request
    d. obedience has most usually paid off in the past

Multiple Choice Answers

1. d (248)   9. d (263)
2. a (249)   10. c (265)
3. d (251)   11. d (268)
4. a (253)   12. d (269)
5. c (254)   13. a (272)
6. d (256)   14. b (274)
7. c (258)   15. c (277)
8. c (261)

Just for Fun: Some Additional Readings

Muson, H.   Moral thinking: Can it be taught?   Psychology Today, Feb.,
    1979.   "There are lots of ways to influence people, but you can't
    influence their moral thinking."   We tend to believe the fore-
    going statement, but there are those who believe that moral
    thinking and decision making can be influenced.

Muson, H.   Blind obedience.   Psychology Today, January, 1978.   This
    article describes a meeting of best minds that have contemplated
    "obedience to authority."   The minds of Stanley Milgram, John
    Dean, and Thomas Szasz are among those that are explored.

Colman, A.   Flattery won't get you everywhere.   Psychology Today, May,
    1980.   The authors covers the limitations of flattery, including
    when it might backfire.

CHAPTER 8

PROSOCIAL BEHAVIOR

Objectives

1. Define "prosocial behaviors," give examples of real life responses in that category and define both "bystander apathy" as well as "bystander effect."

2. Describe the "seizure study" by Darley and Latane (1968) and outline the decisional steps that must be taken before actual help occurs.

3. Define "diffusion of responsibility," tell how the presence of others can decrease or increase helping and indicate how information that increases competence can increase helping (Pantin and Carver, 1982).

4. Define "fear of blunders," indicate conditions that enhance or lessen it and discuss the Gottlieb and Carver (1980) study involving subjects who would or would not meet fellow bystanders after the experiment.

5. Describe how heredity may influence helping behavior, define "reinforcement theory of prosocial behavior" and indicate the conditions under which relieving the distress of another is reinforcing.

6. Define the "bystander calculus" and describe the Batson et al. (1978) study in which potential helpers were either in hurry or not.

7. Discuss how mood can influence helping behavior (Isen and colleagues), an exception to the positive influence of positive mood, the influence of other or self directed attention and Weiner's (1980) "sequence of thought and emotions."

8. Describe Kohlberg's levels of moral development and their possible influence on helping, how gender of helper and helpee makes a difference in helping behavior and how "fear of embarrassment" and political ideology influence helping.

9. Detail how "need for approval" and "empathy" can influence helping, what can increase and decrease the effects of empathy, and describe the hereditary and environmental contributions to empathy.

10. Indicate how physical-social context, need, attractiveness and sensitivity to covert emotional cues influence helping and describe how self-esteem may play a role in reactions to helping (Fisher et al., 1982).

11. What are possible alternative outcomes for self and victim when one interferes with a wrongdoer? Give some examples of heroic or indifferent behavior in the face of someone's plight.

12. Describe the experiment by Latane and Darley (1970) in which $40 was brazenly stolen from a receptionist's desk and the Schwartz and Gottlieb (1980) study of an "attack" on an ESP "sender."

13. Give the characteristics of people who help under dangerous circumstances and indicate how the seriousness of a crime is related to perceptions of persons who report violators to authorities.

14. Indicate the serious implications of shoplifting, the influences of dress and size of witnesses' home community on reporting crime, how people react to modern surveillance devices, and the influence of reporting of a reminder that one has a duty to report. Also tell how Klentz and Beaman (1981) showed that information about reporting a crime and about social factors that inhibit reporting determine amount of reporting.

15. Tell how Moriarty (1975) staged the theft of a radio to show that prior acceptance of responsibility influences intervention to help a victim of a crime. Are people indifferent to the victims of crime?

16. What did Hassett's (1981) survey reveal about the prevalence of crime among 24,000 Americans? What determines participation in violent and nonviolent crimes, situation or personality? What crime is popular with "mature people" and how do taxpayers behave strangely?

17. Detail how cheating on academic tests harms people and state its prevalence. Indicate the personaltiy traits of cheaters. How did Lueger (1980) show that arousal of adolescent boys during intelligence testing influence cheating? Do threats work to stop cheating?

18. Tell how Heisler (1974) deterred cheating in a college class. How does guilt relate to cheating? Describe the procedure and results of the study by Dienstbier et al. (1980) in which subjects learned to fear either external or internal punishments.

Who Done It?

Credit each of the concepts, theories, critical studies or important ideas listed below to the person or persons associated with each (e.g., item: Id-Ego-Superego; associated person: Freud). The correct answers are on the next page.

1. "seizure study" *Darley & Latane*

2. levels of moral development *Kolberg*

3. first to propose the relationship between mood and helping *Berg*
   behavior

4. ran the "attack on the ESP sender" study *Schwartz & Gottlieb*

5. surveyed 24,000 Americans concerning dishonest behaviors *Hassett*

6. staged the theft of a radio on the beach *Moriarty*

7. had subjects read either an "external guilt" passage or an *Dienstbier*
   "internal guilt" passage

8. proposed a "sequence of thoughts and emotions" leading to *Werner*
   helping or not

Define

Each of the critical concepts listed below have been defined in your textbook. For each provide the definition. Answers are on the next page.

1. bystander apathy *the "arm chair psychologist's" catch phrase for why people don't help others in need*

2. bystander effect - *the inhibitory effect on prosocial behavior caused by the presence of more than one witness*

3. fear of blunders - *fear of being embarrassed if interpreting a situation improperly which inhibits prosocial behavior*

4. need for approval *a characteristic in people that cause them to perform prosocial acts if others are viewing them but not if no one else is around*

5. empathy - *the tendency to respond to the world from the perspective of others*

6. reinforcement theory - *the notion that punishment for not helping and reward for helping increases help rates*

7. negative mood - *can cause more prosocial behavior or less depending on social circumstances*

prosocial behaviors - those acts that help others with no obvious benefit to the person performing them but which involve risk and sacrifice based on ethical considerations

99

8. bystander calculus — *the ratio of costs of helping to rewards for helping*

Who Done It Answers

1. Darley and Latane (289)
2. Kohlberg (298)
3. Isen (296)
4. Schwartz and Gottlieb (306)
5. Hassett (311)
6. Moriarty (311)
7. Dienstbier (314)
8. Weiner (297)

Definitions

bystander apathy 1. "the armchair psychologist" catch phrase for explaining why people don't help when others are in need (289)

bystander effect 2. inhibition of appropriate action in a help-needed situation due the presence of more than one witness (289)

fear of blunders 3. fear that falsely judging a potential help-needed situation to be serious when it is not will lead to embarrassment (292)

need for approval 4. a characteristic of people with a strong desire to please others and win their praise; such people help more when being observed than when not being observed (299)

empathy 5. the tendency to respond to the world from the perspective of others (299)

reinforcement theory 6. the notion that punishment for not helping and rewards for helping increase help rates (294)

negative mood 7. a state in which people may help more than controls or less than controls, depending on the social circumstances (296)

bystander calculus 8. a "ratio" of costs of helping to rewards of helping (295

Matching

This exercise appears on the next page. Match each concept or idea on the left with an identifiying phrase, word, or sentence on the right. Answers appear at the bottom of the page.

100

A. stopping an illegal act
B. popular crime among the "mature"
C. when a crime is obvious
D. incident of cheating among students
E. increases likelihood of helping
F. diffusion of responsibility
G. in helping a stranger
H. interpreting
I. fear of blunders (embarrassment)

_E_ 1. being in a helping study
_G_ 2. one must consider potential harm to oneself
_H_ 3. second decision in the Latane and Darley helping model
_I_ 4. source of tendency to avoid "emergency" interpretation
_C_ 5. nonreporters may have claimed not to have noticed
_D_ 6. better than 60% of those interviewed
_A_ 7. may bring harm to the legal or ethical law breaker
_B_ 8. fraud
_F_ 9. letting others who are present in an emergency aid the victim

Is Something Wrong Here?

For each statement below indicate what is incorrect about the statement if anything. If there is something wrong, answer "yes" and indicate what's wrong. If nothing is wrong, ansewr "no; this one is correct." At the end of this exercise you will find the answers.

wrong
1. When one commits an immoral act there are always costs, but never any benefits.

correct
2. Weiner's (1980) "sequence of thoughts and emotions" refers to internal events that lead to helping or not helping.

wrong
3. Poverty is seen by those on the political _right_ left as due to either fate or the failings of the poor.

correct
4. One instructor deterred cheating by planting a "cheater" among students and "apprehending" him during a test.

wrong
5. Threats are _not_ an effective way to stop cheating.

wrong
6. People are indifferent to victims of crime.

correct
7. People who are relatively insensitive to covert emotional cues displayed by a potential helper are more likely to ask for help.

wrong

8. Heredity has ~~no~~ *an* influence on helping behavior.

correct

9. If the self-esteem of a person in need is threatened, s/he may dislike the helper and the aid, but provide more self-help in the future.

wrong

10. People who are in a negative mood do not help.

wrong

11. Paradoxically, other than the display of cheating behavior, students who cheat tend to be normal, moral, upright people.

Correct

12. Empathy may well be influenced by heredity, but environment (training) also plays a role.

wrong

13. According to Latane and Darley, the first thing one must do in *is to notice the event* order to finally arrive at the point of helping is to decide that some unusual event constitutes an emergency.

wrong

14. The last decision one has to make in the process of aiding in an emergency or a crisis is to <u>assume responsibility</u> for the victim's well being.

Is Something Wrong Here Answers

1. Yes; there are also benefits like what the money one could steal would buy. (312)

2. No; this one is correct. (296)

3. Yes; It is those on the right who are most likely to hold these beliefs about impoverished people. (299)

4. No; this one is correct. (314)

5. Yes; threats may even be counterproductive. (317)

6. Yes; not in general. If the crime is serious, if someone points out the duty to help and if information on helping and why people don't help are available, people tend to help. (308-11)

7. No; this one is correct.(302)

8. Yes; several species of animals show helping behavior, implying such behavior may be influenced by the genes due its survival value. (294)

9. No; this one is correct. (303)

10. Yes; sometimes negative mood inhibits helping, and sometimes it doesn't. (296)

11. Yes; cheaters show inability to delay gratification. (316)

12. No; this one is correct. (300-1)

13. Yes; the first thing one must do is to <u>notice</u> the unusual event. (290)

14. Yes; the last decision is deciding to actually help; assuming responsibility is the third decision. (290)

True-False

Indicate whether each of the following statements is true or false. Correct answers are at the end of this exercise.

1. If people commit themselves to being responsible for someone or something prior to a crisis involving that someone or something, they are more likely to help when the crisis actually occurs.

2. In line with notions of "academic honesty" less than 5% of teenage students responding to a recent survey admitted that they have engaged in cheating behavior.

3. "Grading on the curve" is a good way to cancel out any adverse influences of cheating on noncheating students.

4. Fifth-three percent of those who cheated on some kind of academic project felt guilty.

5. According to one theory relieving the stress of another person is reinforcing (such as pressing a lever to relieve a person from electric shock).

6. Unfortunately, even a cohesive group that has embraced the "Good Samaritan norm" is less likely to provide help than a single individual.

True-False Answers

1. True. (311)

2. False; 62% admitted to cheating. (313)

3. False; cheaters raise the "curve" thus penalizing others. (313)

4. True. (314)

5. True of reinforcement theory. (294)

6. False; the presence of such groups increases the likelihood that help will be provided. (291

Fill-in-the-Blanks

Complete the following statements by filling in the blanks with correct information. The answers are at the end of this exercise.

1. The Latane and Darley _seizure_ study in which subjects heard one another discuss some problems while each occupied an isolation booth (communication was by head phone) probably best illustrates their _diffusion of responsibility_ principle. That principle is "the more people present in an emergency, the less responsibility each has for the well-being of the person involved in the emergency."

2. When a person is in a _good_ mood, there is a strong likelihood s/he will help. However, when in a _negative (bad)_ mood, it is uncertain whether s/he will help.

3. When Latane and Darley (1970) staged the theft of $40 from the desk of a secretary, witnesses who didn't help said "_I didn't see it_" or "_I thought it was an accident_" or "_I thought he was making change_."

4. We tend to think that a person who is always needing help is not very _competent_.

5. Help from a friend or even a stranger can _threaten_ self-esteem.

6. One tends to feel a little bit put down upon receiving aid from someone who is very _similar_ to oneself.

7. Shabbily dressed thieves are _more_ likely to be reported than well dressed violators and people from _urban_ _areas_ areas of the nation are less likely to report than their counterparts.

104

8. Finding a dime in a phone booth may be enough to create a good

    _____*mood*_____, because when Alice Isen's subjects found a

    dime, they were more likely to pick up the contents of a

    _____*dropped folder*_____.

9. Sometimes people don't help because they are afraid of looking

    like a fool should their "emergency" interpretation prove

    incorrect. Their _____*fear of embarrassment*_____ inhibits their

    desire to help.

10. Sometimes there is a "grain of truth" to stereotypes. For

    example, it is the case that when help is needed, it is usually

    _____*males*_____ who help and _____*females*_____

    who receive help.

11. The fact that lone males are most likely to help a distressed

    female who is alone indicates that, in addition to altruism,

    there are _____*self centered reasons*_____ for helping.

12. People are very likely to help if someone among witnesses acts

    as a _____*model of responsibility*_____ by openly

    suggesting that helping is appropriate.

13. _____*Well dressed*_____ persons are more likely to receive a

    dime from _____*well dressed*_____ strangers in an airport, while

    _____*poorly dressed*_____ people are more likely to receive the

    same from _____*poorly dressed*_____ strangers in a bus

    terminal.

Fill-in-the-Blank Answers

1. seizure; diffusion of responsibility (289)
2. good; bad (negative) (296)
3. (ansewrs in any order will do) "I didn't see it." "He was making
    change." "The money got into his pocket by accident." (305)

4. competent (302)
5. threaten   (302)
6. similar   (302)
7. more; urban areas (308)
8. mood; dropped folder (296)
9. fear of embarrassment (299)
10. males; females (299)
11. self-centered reasons (romantic) (299)
12. model of responsibility (309)
13. well dressed; well dressed; poorly dressed; poorly dressed (302)

Multiple Choice

d 1. Prosocial behavior
   a. has no obvious benefits for the person by whom it is performed
   b. may involve risk and sacrifice
   c. is based on ethical standards of behavior
   d. all of the above

b 2. In the "seizure" study
   a. subject first saw the person who would later have a "seizure"
   b. subjects "communicated" with the victim of a "seizure" via an intercom system
   c. subjects were to discuss "modern sexuatily"
   d. all of the above

b 3. Diffusion of responsibility
   a. operates only if a witness to an emergency is alone
   b. involves spreading the responsibility to help among several witnesses to an emergency
   c. explains helping rather than not helping
   d. entails accepting responsibility to help in an emergency

d 4. Among the findings of the Pantin and Carver (1982) two-phase "seizure" study was (were)
   a. the bystander effect occurred for all subjects
   b. subjects who had prior competence training showed the strongest bystander effect
   c. male subjects helped more than female subjects
   d. the effect of competence training disappeared after a six-week lapse

C 5. Altruistic behavior may be inborn because
   a. it produces a feeling of security   c. it has survival value
   b. it strengthens the ego   d. all of the above

b 6. When Batson et al. (1978) had some subjects meeting a deadline and/ or on the way to an important engagement, what did they find with regard to responses to a young man slumped in a doorway?
   a. hurrying to meet a deadline had no influence on helping
   b. helping was lowest in the deadline-important engagement condition
   c. being on the way to an important engagement had no influence on helping
   d. both a and c

a 7. When subjects were made to feel sad because a close friend "was ill and dying"
   a. they were more helpful to a stranger later, if they had focused on their friend's feelings instead of their own
   b. they were more helpful to a stranger later, if they had focused on their own feelings instead of their friend's
   c. they were more helpful to a stranger later, regardless of other factors
   d. they were more helpful to a stranger later, only if they were high on the empathy scale

107

d 8. Kohlberg's stages of moral development include
   a. deep religious conviction
   b. doing the "right thing" to avoid punishment
   c. ability to respond to abstract moral values
   d. both b and c

b 9. Poverty is attributed to
   a. discrimination
   b. the failing of the poor when attributions are made by persons on the political right
   c. lack of opportunity
   d. dominance by certain economic made by persons on the political right

c 10. The observation that newborn infants cry in response to the sound of another infant's crying indicates
   a. empathy is wholly learned
   b. they have poor auditory acuity
   c. empathy may be in part inborn
   d. that they are unable to differentiate between their own crying and that of other infants

a 11. From whom is one most likely to seek aid?
   a. an unattractive person   c. a religious person
   b. a handicapped person   d. a short person

d 12. A 25-year-old obstetrics nurse ran along a busy street pleading to be saved from an assailant
   a. one witness peered out a window at the victim, then went back to her chores
   b. as she ran down the street, a delivery man swerved to miss her and kept on going
   c. she begged for help from a man in a parked car; he drove away
   d. all of the above

b 13. Among the procedures of the Schwartz and Gottlieb (1980) "ESP" experiment were (was)
   a. a stranger entered the subject's room and proceeded to steal the latter's belongings
   b. a stranger entered the sender's room, picked up the latter's calculator and attempted to walk out with it
   c. after completing a questionnaire, each subject left, only to find a young man slumped in the hallway
   d. the subject watched an ESP sender via a TV monitor; after a time, the sender began to have a "seizure"

c 14. The more serious the crime, the
   a. the less moral is the act of reporting it
   b. the more immoral is the act of reporting it
   c. the more moral is the act of reporting it
   d. the more morally indifferent is the act of reporting it

15. Which of the following is likely to increase the likelihood of actual helping?
    a. a lecture on the sorry state of human nature
    b. receiving information about factors that lead to helping
    c. hearing a lecture exhorting people to help fellow humans trouble
    d. all of the above are equally likely to increase helping

16. In the "prior commitment" condition of Moriarty's (1975) study, what percentage of subjects took action?
    a. 95   c. 43
    b. 25   d. 62

17. What crime is particularly popular among "mature" persons
    a. blackmail   c. fraud
    b. confidence game   d. petty larceny

Multiple Choice Answers

1. d (287)   10. c (300)
2. b (289)   11. a (302)
3. b (290)   12. d (305)
4. d (291)   13. b (306)
5. c (294)   14. c (306)
6. b (296)   15. b (309)
7. a (296)   16. a (311)
8. d (298)   17. c (313)
9. b (299)

Just for Fun: Some Additional Readings

Huston, T., Geis, G., and Wright, R. The angry Samaritans. *Psychology Today*, June, 1976. Are all Good Samaritans good at heart? Not necessarily, according to this article. Some people "help" because they like violence, taking a chance and seeing their name in newspapers.

Takooshian, H., Haber, S., and Lucido, D. Who wouldn't help a lost child? *Psychology Today*, February, 1977. Some people may be callous, but surely even the most unfeeling person would stop to help a lost child. Right? Wrong! A lost child is in big trouble, especially in the big city.

Peoria Journal Star, Baloon blast kills 4 people, October 4, 1982, (p. 1). A hot-air balloon is on fire. People are jumping from it. Incredibly, as the ballon reaches 50 feet, a woman rushes to catch a child who is about to jump. She ignores the fact that she would be crushed by the falling body. She is tackled by her husband.

CHAPTER 9

AGGRESSION: ITS NATURE, CAUSES, AND CONTROL

Objectives:

1. Define aggression and consider the following qualifications:
    behavioral in nature, intended, directed toward living beings,
    and victims who are motivated to avoid harm.

2. Describe the "instinct" theories of Freud and Lorenz, including
    the circularity of this position, and indicate the basic
    principles of "sociobiology."

3. Describe the "drive" theories of aggression, especially
    "frustration-aggression."

4. Define "social learning" and give the three main issues that
    must be addressed if aggression is to be understood. Compare
    this point of view with the others, indicating how optimistic
    each is with regard to controlling and preventing aggression.

5. Deal with the issues of studying aggression, such as deception,
    the variations in methods of "hurting" people in aggression
    experiments, the Buss method, including the two "cover stories"
    used with it, and the evidence that the methods of studying
    aggression actually address real aggression.

6. What were the original assumptions behind the "frustration-
    aggression" hypothesis? Indicate the variety of reactions to
    frustration, reasons for attacking people other than frustra-
    tion, when frustration might lead to facilitation of aggres-
    sion, and the variety of influences that frustration has been
    shown to exert on aggression.

7. Indicate the importance of provocation in promoting aggression
    and outline the role of attributions of intention to harm doers
    in determining reactions by victims.

8. Define "aggressive model" and consider the famous "Bobo doll" studies as well as criticisms of the same.

9. Indicate the alternate, laboratory method of studying the impact of "media" models on children's aggression and results of research using that method.

10. Use the study by Leyens and colleagues (1975) as an example of how the effects of "media" models can be long-term. Also, indicate how Eron and colleagues showed how models on television influence aggression both in the short and long term and for countries other than the U.S.

11. Tell how exposure to violence on television can yield aggression in viewers by attention to "weakening of inhibitions," the acquisition of new forms of aggression and the desensitization of viewers to aggression. Also, note qualifications to the link between TV viewing and aggression.

12. Describe the evidence that "excitation transfer" underlies the influence of arousal on aggression, with attention to "residual arousal" and whether arousal is attributed to provocation or to some other source.

13. Discuss the older conceptions of the possible link between aggression and sexual arousal, results of early studies, the importance of whether sexual displays are explicit, and the critical nature of the level of arousal and the kinds of feelings generated by sexual stimuli.

14. What is the new trend in sexual displays in the media and what implications does it have for the way women are viewed? Describe the study by Donnerstein and Berkowitz (1981) in which there were "positive" and negative outcomes of rape. Discuss the overall effect of exposure to violent and non-violent pornography.

15. Define "aggressive cues," give examples, and indicate other determinants of aggression. Illustrate "aggressive personalities" and discuss the two individual difference factors that have been shown to influence aggressiveness (other than sex and XYY).

16. Who is most likely to commit violent crimes, men or women and who has been shown to be more aggressive in the lab, according to the older studies? List and discuss the two factors that may account for recent results that contradict the early findings on sex differences, with emphasis on Richardson and colleagues' (1981) "reaction time" study.

17. Indicate the early conclusions concerning the influence of the XYY configuration on aggressiveness and follow with a description of the study in Denmark by Witkin and colleagues (1976). What did the latter suggest is the real culprit behind the XYY-criminal behavior link?

18. List the conditions under which punishment can be expected to deter or prevent aggression, and the degree these conditions are met in reality. In what two ways may a punisher increase the aggressiveness of his victim?

19. State the "catharsis" hypothesis and indicate what two effects catharsis is supposed to have. Indicate the limited conditions for which catharsis might work to reduce aggression and the three circumstances for which it has been shown not to work. What are three reasonable conclusions about "catharsis?"

20. Tell what influence nonaggressive models have on aggression and how such models might be exploited in real situations. The lack of which trainable social skills seems to predispose people to aggression? Tell how alerting victims of provocation to "mitigating circumstances" that may explain an aggressor's behavior can lower the likelihood of retaliation, with emphasis on Kremer and Stephans (1983) involving the "rude experimenter."

21. Define "incompatible responses" and list three sources of such responses that may deter aggression. State three reasons why the "incompatible responses" strategy for reducing aggression may have great practical utility. Indicate three real life contexts in which incompatible responses may be especially useful in the prevention of aggression. For one of them, rape, give examples of how the method has actually worked.

Who Done It?

Credit each of the concepts, theories, critical studies or important ideas listed below to the person or persons associated with each (e.g., item: Id-Ego-Superego; associated person: Freud). The correct answers are on the next page.

1. Danish XYY survey _Witkin_

2. death instinct _Freud_

3. fighting instinct _Lorenz_

4. the study involving "positive" and "negative" outcomes of rape _Donnerstein & Berkowitz_

5. rude experimenter study _Kremer and Stephens_

6. inventor of the aggression machine _Buss_

Who Done It Answers

1. Witkin (351)
2. Freud (327)
3. Lorenz (328)

4. Donnerstein and Berkowitz (346)
5. Kremer and Stephens (358)
6. Buss (333)

Define

Each of the critical concepts listed below have been defined in your textbook. For each provide the definition. The answers are at the bottom of the page.

1. intention — *a necessary element for an act of harm to another to be considered aggression*

2. sociobiology — *holds that aggression is innate or genetically "programmed."*

3. social learning — *a theory that holds that aggression is form of social behavior which is acquired and maintained in the same manner as other social behaviors*

4. aggressive cues — *Berkowitz's notion that certain objects or entities act as cues for aggressive act eg. guns*

5. XY — *the normal male chromosome pattern*

6. "mitigating circumstances" — *factors that explain why an aggressor provokes a victim*

7. catharsis — *the belief that committing aggressive acts directly or vicariously leads to a lowering of aggression on future occasions.*

8. empathy — *fitting into someone else's shoes, feeling as they do.*

9. *Aggression is any form of behavior aimed at the goal of hurting or injuring another live recipient who is motivated to avoid it*

Definitions

1. necessary element of an act ending in harm to someone if that act is to be labeled "aggression" (325)

2. a new discipline in biology holding that aggression is innate or genetically "programmed" (328)

3. a theory that regards aggression mainly as a specific form of social behavior, a form that is both acquired and maintained in much the same manner as many other forms of social behavior (329)

4. Berkowitz's notion that certain objects or entities act as cues for aggressive acts; e.g., guns (345)

5. normal male human chromosomal pattern (351)

6. factors that explain to a victim why an aggressor has provoked her (357)

7. the belief that committing aggressive acts directly or vicariously leads to a lowering of aggression on future occasions (354)

8. fitting into someone else's shoes; feeling as they do (359)

Matching

Match each concept on the left with an identifying phrase, word or sentence on the right. The answers are at the bottom of the page.

A. not really aggression
B. drive theory of aggression
C. incompatible responses
D. Richardson et al.'s "reaction time study"
E. determines whether harm is seen as aggression
F. temporary deception about experiment
G. frustration-aggression theory

G 1. frustration always leads to aggression
D 2. no sex difference with strong provocation
B 3. internal elicited pressures toward harm to others
F 4. cover stories
A 5. attacks against inanimate object
C 6. responses that exclude acts of aggression
E 7. attribution of intention to harm doer

Is Something Wrong Here?

For each statement below indicate what is incorrect about the statement if anything. If there is something wrong, answer "yes" and indicate what's wrong. If nothing is wrong, answer "no; this one is correct." At the end of this exercise you will find the answers.

wrong
1. "Blowing off steam," for example, yelling at someone, seems to drain off aggression. *it isn't clear that it does*

correct
2. Exhausting exercises may reduce arousal that is due to strong provocation.

correct
3. Threat of punishment may "work" to reduce aggressive tendencies, if the punishment is severe, immediate, and highly likely to occur.

Matching Answers

1. G 331
2. D 349
3. B 328
4. F 332
5. A 326
6. C 358
7. E 335

wrong

4. "Sexy" jokes tend to ~~increase~~ *decrease* the likelihood of aggression.

correct *if they lack aggressive content*

5. In the typical aggression experiment, subjects receive a sample electric shock.

wrong *there are other outlets for frustration*

6. Frustration always leads to aggression.

correct

7. The lack of certain social skills can dispose a person to aggressiveness.

correct

8. Research shows that incompatible responses can be highly effective in reducing aggression even in extremely angry individuals.

correct

9. A major difference between XYYs and "normals" is that XYYs tend to have lower I.Q. scores.

wrong

10. Contrary to evidence from other sub-disciplines of psychology, "modeling" seemed to be an unimportant factor in human aggression.

correct

11. With sufficiently strong provocation, sex differences in aggressiveness disappear.

correct

12. "Hurting the one who hurt you" seems to describe the only case whereby aggressing against someone cathartically may decrease subsequent aggression.

correct

13. Individuals who deliver punishment may be seen as aggressive models by those who receive it.

wrong

14. "Residual arousal" is the arousal that occurs ~~right~~ after some event like physical exercise. *and continues for some time*

correct

15. Investigations of the relationship between exposure to erotica and subsequent aggressiveness have yielded mixed results.

correct

16. Among the characteristics peculiar to individuals that may predict their level of aggressiveness are specific personality traits.

correct

17. Instinct theories are circular in nature.

wrong

18. Contrary to popular belief, women are almost as likely to commit violent crimes as are men. *not according to prison population*

Is Something Wrong Here? Answers

1. Yes; it may even work the other way around. (355)

2. No; this one is correct. (355)

3. No; this one is correct. (353)

116

4. Yes; "sexy" jokes are likely to decrease aggression, if they lack aggressive content. (359)

5. No; this one is correct. (333)

6. Yes; while it may sometimes, it doesn't necessarily. There are other outlets for frustration. (334)

7. No; this one is correct. (356)

8. No; this one is correct. (360)

9. No; this one is correct. (351)

10. Yes; aggressive models increase aggressive behavior. (337)

11. No; this one is correct. (350)

12. No; this one is correct. (335)

13. No; this one is correct. (353)

14. Yes; residual arousal is left over some time after exercise. (342)

15. No; this one is correct. (343)

16. No; this one is correct. (348)

17. No; this one is correct. (328)

18. Yes; check the prison population. (349)

True-False

Indicate whether each of the following statements is true or false. Correct answers are at the end of this exercise.

F 1. Aggression is a kind of internal state as opposed to a kind of behavior.

F 2. In order to determine whether aggression has occurred, it is only necessary to determine that one person has hurt another person.

T 3. Although it may be surprising to some people, aggression is learned, at least in the case of humans.

T 4. Boxers and soldiers are examples of persons who aggress although they do not do so primarily because of frustration.

T 5. Bobo dolls have frequently been used in the study of "aggression."

F 6. Provocation seems to be infrequently necessary for aggression to occur.

T 7. In some aggression experiments, subjects aggress by writing evaluations of the person who provoked them.

F 8. The presention of erotica has only one influence on aggression; it increases aggression.

T 9. If subjects see their behavior in an aggression experiment as intentional harm doing, it can properly be called "aggression."

T 10. Heat and crowding are factors influencing aggression that are covered in other chapters.

F 11. In "excitation transfer" arousal due to aggression is transferred to some other activity.

T 12. If a potential rape victim can arouse incompatible responses in a rapist, she may escape harm.

True-False Answers

1. False; aggression is a kind of behavior. (325)

2. False; it is also necessary to establish whether the "hurt" was intentional. (325)

3. True. (329)

4. True. (334)

5. True. (337)

6. False; it is almost always necessary. (335)

7. True. (333)

8. False; mild erotica decreases aggression while strong erotica increases it. (343)

9. True. (333)

10. True. (345)

11. False; it is the other way around. (341)

12. True. (361)

Fill-in-the-Blanks

Complete the following statements by filling in the blanks with correct information. The answers are at the end of this exercise.

1. Attacking persons who enjoy being hurt does not qualify as _aggression_ .

2. _sociobiological_ and _Freudian_ points of view are pessimistic concerning the possibility of controlling aggression.

3. _Social learning theory_ is optimistic with regard to controlling aggression.

4. According to the frustration-aggression theory, frustration is supposed to increase aggressive _drive_ .

5. The _"teacher - learner" setup_ is among the popular means of studying human aggression.

6. An alternative way to study aggression involves the "measuring of _physiological_ responses" cover story.

7. Television can lead to aggression in viewers by fostering a weakening of _inhibitions_ .

8. Viewing TV violence is _unlikely_ to cause a person to go out and commit an act of violence.

9. _Excitation transfer_ refers to the transfer of excitation from its original source to feelings of anger.

10. "Desensitization" to TV violence means that frequent viewers of violence will show a _reduced_ reaction to aggression displayed on television.

Fill-in-the-Blank Answers

1. aggression (326)
2. sociobiological, Freudian (or Lorcuzian) (326)
3. social learning theory (330)

4. drive (331)
 5. "teacher-learner" setup (333)
 6. physiological (333)
 7. inhibitions (340)
 8. unlikely (341)
 9. "Excitation transfer" (342)
10. reduced (340)

Multiple Choice

1. Aggression is any form of _____ directed toward the goal of harming or injuring another living being who is motivated to avoid such treatment. (Fill in the blank with the correct answer)
   a. emotion
   b. thought
   c. behavior
   d. instinct

2. If the definition of aggression didn't specify the target of aggression as a "living being," which of the following would be considered aggression?
   a. kicking a can
   c. cursing the "gods"
   c. hitting a bobo doll
   d. all of the above

3. The contention that aggressive behavior is genetically programmed is made by
   a. sociobiologists
   b. Freudians
   b. anthropologists
   d. psychologists

4. According to what theory would the elimination of aggression be accomplished by the elimination of pain and thwarting of goal attainment?
   a. sociobiological
   b. attitudinal
   c. frustration-aggression
   d. absolutional

5. Compared with Freud as well as Lorenz and the sociobiologists, social learning theorists are relatively _____ about the control of aggressiveness (fill in the blank).
   a. pessimistic
   b. indifferent
   c. optimistic
   d. sophisticated

6. What is the dilemma of studying human aggression?
   a. to study it is to condone it
   b. to study it you must make people aggress and, thereby, you are contributing to the growing problem of aggression
   c. how does one study aggression without harming someone?
   d. how can one study aggression without drawing moral conclusions?

7. Which of the following regularly show aggression though they are not frustrated?
   a. boxers
   b. minority persons
   c. persons who have just lost their jobs
   d. persons who are deeply religious

8. If a person is hurt by another person, what must the first person determine before deciding how to respond to the second person?
   a. nothing, retaliation is automatic
   b. nothing, most people are civilized and don't retaliate regardless of circumstances
   c. whether or not the second person intended to hurt him/her
   d. whether the second person is physically stronger or weaker than is he/she

121

9. Problems with the "Bobo Doll" studies can be solved by
   a. using dolls that are representations of humans
   b. using real people as the targest of humans
   c. using only adults as subjects
   d. doing the research in laboratory settings

10. Earlier studies investigating exposure to erotica and aggression can be characterized as
    a. clear-cut; erotica and aggression are unrelated
    b. clear-cut; erotica and aggression are positively related (the former increases the latter)
    c. mixed; some studies showed a positive relationship between exposure to erotica and aggression and some a negative relationship
    d. mixed; some studies showed a relationship between erotica and aggression and others showed no relationship

11. Two types of "post-Bobo doll" studies have been done to investigate the influence of witnessing violence on subsequent aggression. Which of the following represents one of those types of studies?
    a. watching adult models throw marshmallows at a panda-bear doll
    b. children watching the "Untouchables" and then having the opportunity to inflict pain on another child
    c. children watch other children throw darts at a target shaped like a human body and then have their own opportunity to throw the darts
    d. children watch the "Road Runner" aggress against the "Coyote" and then draw pictures that are analyzed for aggressive content

12. "The next time that bully bothers me, I'll use Captain America's moves on the so-and-so," indicates which of the following effects?
    a. desensitization
    b. acquisition of novel forms of aggression
    c. weakening of inhibitions
    d. trivilization of violence

13. Donnerstein and Berkowitz (1981) had subjects view films. What did they find?
    a. compared to the control film, both experimental films increased aggression against the female accomplice
    b. nonangered subjects showed enhancement of aggression against the female accomplice only if she "enjoyed" her mistreatment
    c. angered subjects showed enhancement of aggression against the female accomplice only if she "enjoyed" her mistreatment
    d. nonangered subjects showed enhancement of aggression against the female accomplice only if she showed suffering during her ordeal

122

14. What individual factors, other than sex and XYY, have been shown   *a*
    to influence aggression?
    a. specific personality traits
    b. low blood pressure
    c. type of reinforcement used by parents
    d. all of the above

15. Richardson and colleagues (1983) had males and females compete in   *c*
    the "reaction time game." Their procedure included
    a. the use of aversive noise
    b. competition on only one trial
    c. subjects "losing" on 50% of the trials
    d. the use of negative ratings as the form of aggression

16. When Witkins and his colleageus did a survey of Danish men, they
    found that people with a rare chromosome pattern which is found   *d*
    more frequently among prisoners
    a. are naturally prone to violence
    b. are more likely to get caught than others
    c. are less intelligent than others
    d. both b and c

Multiple Choice Answers

1.	c (325)	9.	b (338)
2.	d (326)	10.	c (343)
3.	a (328)	11.	b (338)
4.	c (329)	12.	b (340)
5.	c (330)	13.	b (346)
6.	c (332)	14.	a (348)
7.	a (331)	15.	c (349)
8.	c (335)	16.	d (351)

Just for Fun: Additional Readings

Newsweek, "The Warriors" body count, Feb., 26, 1979. There is much controversy as to whether depictions of violence in the media incite violence in media audiences. Score one for those who believe that media violence causes real life violence. Several attackes, including at least one ending in a fatality, were directly linked to screenings of the movie, "The Warriors."

Bingham, R. Trivers in Jamaica. Science 80, March/April, 1980. Sociobiologists are supposed to believe that aggression and other forms of social behavior are determined by the genes. Such people are often called "racist" because they are accused of explaining "racial differences" that are presumed to exist as "genetic" in nature and thus unchangeable. If all this is true, Robert Trivers is certainly an enigma. This white sociobiologist is married to a black woman and is a member of the Black Panthers.

Tavris, C. Anger/defused. Psychology Today, November, 1982. Tavris reviews her book and convincingly argues that catharsis doesn't work to make you healthy. Expressing aggression only makes matters worse.

Berkowitz, L. How guns controls us. Psychology Today, June, 1981. Armed with new evidence, Berkowitz argues that "aggressive cues" such as guns increase the likelihood of violence.

Leo, J. and Crane, T. Deadly dilemma for women. Newsweek, Sept. 21, 1981. Whether to fight or play for time, that is the question facing women who worry about confronting a rapist. There are plenty of self-defense classes, but is violence the way to counter violence?

CHAPTER 10

SOCIAL EXCHANGE: COMING TO TERMS WITH OTHERS

Objectives

money, love, service, information, goods, status

1. List Foa's six exchanged resources, the two dimensions on which these vary, and note the reciprocity tendency.

2. Describe the "Prisoner's Dilemma" and how it is used by social psychologists.

3. Summarize the reciprocity principle, and note the conditions that cause exploitation.

4. How do attributions affect cooperation/competition, and how does behavior affect attributions?

5. Summarize the findings regarding the effects of group size on cooperation   Why does cooperation decline with increased size?

6. List the advantages and disadvantages of breaking groups into subgroups.

7. Summarize the goals and behaviors of competitors, cooperators, and individualists.

8. Compare the social exchange outcomes of Type As and Type Bs.

9. What effect does the availability of an alternative have on bargaining?

10. Under what circumstances does communication help vs. hinder bargainers?

11. Explain how each of the following strategies is used to resolve conflicts:
    a) The GRIT approach
    b) Problem-solving orientation
    c) Third-party intervention

12. Compare the success of high and low Machs in social exchange.

13. Summarize the rule of distributive justice (or "equity").

14. How is people's judgment of what's fair affected by egocentrism?

15. What are the circumstances under which an equality rule is followed?

16. How are outcomes distributed when a relative needs rule is used?

17. What circumstances affect whether equality or equity is followed?

18. What are the four strategies that people use to eliminate feelings of unfairness?

19. List the six suggestions for maximizing positive outcomes in social exchange.

20. When does relative deprivation generate resentment?

Who Done It?

Credit each of the concepts, theories, critical studies or important ideas listed below to the person or persons associated with each (e.g., item: Id-Ego-Superego; associated person: Freud). Answers are on the next page.

1. divided exchanged resources into six categories   *Foa*

2. study showing that people expect their partner to respond as they do in social exchange   *Messé and Sivacek*

3. study showing that cooperation declines as group size increases and that simply dividing into subgroups does not help much   *Komorita & Lapworth*

4. study comparing expectations of Type As vs. Type Bs in game-playing   *Gotay*

5. study showing that having an alternative is a big advantage to bargainers   *Komorita, Lapworth & Lumann*

6. study showing that the <u>timing</u> of a communication determines its effect on bargaining   *Heck & McClintock*

7. study showing that high Machs are skilled deceivers   *Davis & Moon*

8. study examining effects of self-awareness and expectations about meeting partner on equity/equality payment   *Greenberg*

126

Who Done It Answers

1. Foa (368)
2. Messé and Sivacek (376)
3. Komorita and Lapworth (378)
4. Gotay (381)
5. Komorita, Lapworth, and Lumonis (385)
6. Stech and McClintock (388)
7. Geis and Moon (393)
8. Greenberg (399)

Define

Each of the critical concepts listed below have been defined in your textbook. For each provide the definition. Answers are on the next page.

1. cooperation — *when 2 or more individuals work together and coordinate their actions to obtain a common goal*
2. competition — *when individuals seek to obtain a better outcome than their partner*
3. social exchange situations — *those situations in which individuals trade or exchange something tangible or intangible with others*
4. principle of reciprocity — *the principle of behaving toward others so you would like them to behave toward you*
5. bargaining — *a form of social exchange in which mutual exchange or trading of offers with possible concessions take place*
6. Machiavellianism — *a personality dimension that deals with how one affects others and is affected by them in social exchange*
7. equity — *a rule for dividing rewards in the exchange relationship based on each one receiving reward in proportion to contribution*

Matching

Match each concept or idea on the left with an identifying phrase, word or sentence on the right. Answers are on the next page.

A. Type A person
B. "Loss of face"
C. GRIT approach
D. high Mach
E. equity
F. exploitation
G. entrapping conflicts
H. attribution
I. bargainer's advantage

_F_ 1. response to unconditionally cooperative partner
_D_ 2. skilled at influencing, resistant to being influenced
_H_ 3. answers <u>why</u> partner is cooperating
_G_ 4. trying to justify past costs
_I_ 5. having an alternative
_B_ 6. backing down to partner's threat causes this
_C_ 7. Kennedy's 1963 decision to stop nuclear testing
_E_ 8. rule of distributive justice
_A_ 9. they push themselves to the limit

127

Definitions

1. two or more individuals work together or coordinate their actions to obtain some goal (370)

2. individuals in an exchange relationship seek to obtain better outcomes than their partner (370)

3. situations in which two or more persons trade or exchange something; the thing traded may be tangible or intangible, and thus some theorists view virtually all relationships to be of this type (368)

4. behaving toward others as they've behaved toward us (374)

5. a form of social exchange, in which people engage in a mutual trading of offers and perhaps concessions (382)

6. a personality dimension related to how one affects others and is affected by them in social exchange relationships (393)

7. a rule for dividing rewards in an exchange relationship; states that persons should receive outcomes that match their contributions (395

Matching Answers

1. F (375) 6. B (387)
2. D (392) 7. C (389)
3. H (375) 8. E (395)
4. G (382) 9. A (381)
5. I (385)

Is Something Wrong Here?

For each statement below indicate what is wrong about the statement, if anything. If there is something wrong, answer "yes" and indicate what's wrong. If nothing is wrong, answer "no; this one is correct." At the end of this exercise you will find the answers.

1. In the Shure, Meeker, and Hansford (1965) study, the way subjects responded to an unconditionally cooperative partner was by reciprocating cooperation.

2. The effect of communications that occur ~~early~~ in bargaining is more positive than for those that occur ~~late~~ in bargaining.

3. Individuals who are threatened by their opponents in a bargaining context usually respond with ~~submission.~~

128

wrong

4. In the graduated reciprocation of tension reduction strategy, the initial move involves the bargainers' making a mutual trading of offers or concessions before they publicly announce their final agreement. *One bargainer makes a small unilateral concession*

correct

5. Mediation seems to be more effective when the conflict between the opposing sides is large because each side can make concessions without losing face.

correct

6. The Mach Scale is a personality test that measures characteristics important in domination and control of social interactions.

wrong

7. The person who shows cool detachment, is highly resistant to social influence, and skilled at influencing others is a ~~low~~ *high* Mach.

wrong | *High*

8. ~~Low~~ *High* Machs are perceived to be more truthful than ~~high~~ *low* Machs.

wrong

9. Greenberg's (1983) subjects followed the rule of ~~equity~~ *equality* when they anticipated meeting their low-performing partner.

Is Something Wrong Here Answers

1. Yes; subjects <u>exploited</u> the unconditionally cooperative partner. (385)

2. Yes; communications that occur <u>late</u> produce a more positive effect. (387)

3. Yes; people respond with anger and a stiffened resistance. (387)

4. Yes; the initial move occurs when one party makes a small unilateral concession in order to put pressure on the opponent to do the same. (389)

5. No, this one is correct. (391)

6. No, this one is correct. (392)

7. Just the opposite; the person described is a high Mach. (393)

8. Yes; high Machs are perceived to be more truthful, and the difference is especially large when the person is telling a lie. (393)

9. Yes; they followed the rule of equality in this conditions because of their desire to make a favorable impression. (399)

Indicate whether each of the following statements is true or false. Correct answers are at the end of the exercise.

_T_ 1. Goods are higher in concreteness than information.

_T_ 2. Information is low on both particularism and concreteness.

_F_ 3. When engaging in social exchange, people seldom return the same type of resource that they have received.

_T_ 4. The most important reason why people often fail to cooperate is that the goals they seek simply can't be shared.

_T_ 5. When one person cooperates and the other competes in the prisoner's dilemma game, the cooperating person receives the better outcome.

_T_ 6. As the number of persons participating in a social exchange rises, the level of cooperation often decreases.

_F_ 7. There are no differences in the behavior of cooperators, competitors, and individualists in the prisoner's dilemma game.

_F_ 8. For purposes of maximizing one's eventual outcome, the best strategy for a bargainer is to demonstrate good faith by making a moderate initial offer.

_T_ 9. Having a viable alternative is an advantage to a bargainer.

_T_ 10. High Machs generally receive better outcomes in social exchange relationships than low Machs.

_F_ 11. Individuals who witness another person receiving unfair electric shocks have been found to increase their liking for this individual because of their feeling of sympathy.

True-False Answers

1. True (368)

2. True (368)

3. False; they generally return the same type they've received. (369)

4. True (370)

5. False; the person who <u>competes</u> receives the better outcome. (371)

6. True (377)

130

7. False; each displays behavior that is consistent with what we'd expect. (380)

8. False; extreme initial offers enhance one's eventual outcomes. One must be careful not to elicit anger or withdrawal with the initial offer, however. (383)

9. True (385)

10. True (393)

11. False; people tend to perceive that the person deserves the treatment, and they derogate the person as part of the process. (402)

Fill-in-the-Blanks

Complete the following statements by filling in the blanks with correct information. The answers are at the end of this exercise.

1. List Foa's six basic categories of exchanged resources:

    1) _*love*_ ; 2) _*status*_ ; 3) _*information*_ ;

    4) _*money*_ ; 5) _*goods*_ ; and 6) _*services*_ .

2. When the value of an exchanged resource is heavily influenced by who delivers it, the resource is high on _*particularism*_ .

3. When an exchanged resource must take a specific form to be of value, the resource is high on _*concreteness*_ .

4. When we behave toward others as they have behaved toward us, our behavior is following the principle of _*reciprocity*_ .

5. Our tendency to view our own behavior as typical is termed _*the false consensus effect*_ .

6. Countering selfish behavior in large groups by dividing the group into subgroups seems to fail because of our tendency to perceive members of other groups as _*out group members*_ .

7. The best strategy for developing cooperation among the members of a large group is to divide into smaller units and remind the members of _*superordinate*_ goals.

8. People who seek to maximize their own gains <u>relative</u> to other people are _competitors_; people who seek to maximize their own gains <u>and</u> those of others are _cooperators_ people who are concerned with maximizing their own gains, without concern for others, are _individualist_.

9. The personality type characterized by competitiveness, a sense of time urgency, and a relatively high probability of a serious heart attack is _Type A_.

10. The technique for resolving interpersonal conflict in which both sides are encouraged to find an agreement that is acceptable to all is _the problem-solving orientation_.

11. When a persistent conflict is resolved by a third party who can merely suggest terms of the agreement, the technique is _mediation_; when the third party can dictate the terms of the agreement, the technique is _arbitration_.

12. The _equity_ rule states that fairness exists when the ratio of person A's outcomes and contributions is approximately equal to the ratio of person B's outcomes and contributions.

13. _Egocentrism_ is the form of bias that leads us to favor ourselves in terms of what we perceive to be a fair share of available rewards.

14. We tend to perceive our successful behavior as stemming from _internal_ causes and our unsuccessful behavior as stemming from _external_ causes.

15. In addition to the equity rule, other rules used in making judgments of fairness include _equality_ and _relative need_.

132

16. We use the _equality_ rule when our goal is to induce others to have positive feelings toward us; we use the _equity_ rule when our goal is to enhance our own self-image.

17. In the Greenberg (1983) study, subjects who were made self-aware and did not expect to meet their low-performing partner followed the _equity_ rule.

18. The four strategies that people employ to eliminate feelings of unfairness in an exchange relationship are: 1) _altering contributions_; 2) _altering outcomes_; 3) _withdrawing from the relationship_; and 4) _changing one's perception_.

19. The tendency of persons receiving more than they deserve to devalue the persons they exploit is known as _victim degradation_.

20. When individuals desire benefits they do not now enjoy, perceive that others possess them, and feel that they too are entitled to them, feelings of _relative deprivation_ are often aroused.

Fill-in-the-Blank Answers

1. love; status; information; money; goods; services (368)
2. particularism (368)
3. concreteness (368)
4. reciprocity (374)
5. the false consensus effect (377)
6. out-group members (377)
7. superordinate (379)
8. competitors; cooperators; individualists (380)
9. Type A (381)
10. the problem-solving orientation (390)
11. mediation; arbitration (390)
12. equity (395)
13. Egocentrism (396)
14. internal; external (396)
15. equality; relative needs (397)
16. equality; equity (398)
17. equity (399)

18. altering contributions; altering outcomes; withdrawing from the relationship; changing one's perception (400)
19. victim derogation (402)
20. relative deprivation (404)

Multiple Choice

1. An example of an exchanged resource which is high on particularism
   is
   a. love
   b. goods
   c. services
   d. money
   e. b, c, and d

   a

2. Cooperation is (by definition) beneficial to all persons involved.
   Why, then, doesn't it develop in most, if not all, situations?
   a. because human beings are irrational creatures, who often be-
      have in ways contrary to their own best interests
   b. because the lure of competition is so great that many people
      can't resist it
   c. because most people are selfish, and can't stand sharing
      rewards with others
   d. because many goals sought by several persons can't be shared
      among them

   d

3. What role does attribution play in social exchange (e.g., cooperation and competition)?
   a. very little; social perception is largely unrelated to this
      process
   b. it plays an important role, since we always want to know why
      other people are cooperating or competing with us
   c. it influences cooperation, but not competition
   d. none of the above

   b

4. Our tendency to view our own behavior as typical is termed
   a. reciprocity
   b. the reciprocal attribution effect
   c. the false consensus effect
   d. the social averaging effect

   c

5. What is the best strategy for developing cooperation among the
   members of a large group?
   a. simply dividing the large group into smaller units should be
      sufficient
   b. divide the large group into smaller units and remind the
      members of superordinate goals
   c. divide the large group into smaller units and allow the
      smaller units to develop strong "in-group" feelings
   d. divide the large group into smaller units that are clearly
      different from each other in status

   b

6. Which of the following is not characteristic of Type A person?
   a. they are competitive
   b. they feel a sense of time urgency
   c. they are easy-going and friendly
   d. they have a relatively high likelihood of suffering a serious
      heart attack

   c

7. What strategy would be most effective for a real-estate broker who wants to obtain the maximum possible price for a house?
   a. begin with an offer that is extreme, so that the buyer will lower her expectations
   b. begin with a moderate offer, so as to demonstrate "good faith"
   c. begin with a low offer, so that the buyer will be interested
   d. begin with an offer which is so extreme that it angers the buyer

8. Bargainers demand a larger proportion of an available prize when they are the _____ player and there is an alternative with a _____ probability.
   a. weak; high
   b. strong; high
   c. weak; low
   d. strong; low

9. Consider a communication between bargainers that occurred early, was delivered face-to-face, and contained threats. Of the underlined factors, which would be expected to hinder the bargaining process?
   a. the fact that it contained threats
   b. the fact that it was early and contained threats
   c. the fact that it was delivered face-to-face and contained threats
   d. all of the underlined factors would hinder bargaining

10. When bargaining fails, one strategy for reducing tension and conflict is to adopt
   a. a problem-solving orientation
   b. a Machiavellian approach
   c. an extreme position
   d. a baby chimpanzee

11. People who obtain _____ scores on the Mach scale generally achieve the best outcomes in social exchange.
   a. high
   b. low
   c. medium
   d. none of the above, since one's Mach score is unrelated to social exchange

12. Which of the following is not one of the factors that makes high Mach subjects successful in social exchange?
   a. their capacity to avoid emotional involvement
   b. their honesty
   c. their effective use of deception
   d. their ability to use social influence on others
   e. both a and c

13. In order to decide whether a social exchange is fair or not, individuals rely on several different rules or standards. One of these requires that all participants in an exchange receive outcomes proportional to their inputs. This rule is known as
   a. equality
   b. relative needs
   c. equity
   d. justice

136

14. Which is (are) an indication of our tendency to engage in ego-
centric thinking?   *d*
    a. we demand a larger share of rewards for ourselves than we
       deserve
    b. we react more negatively to being shortchanged than we do to
       receiving more than we deserve
    c. inequity that involves us directly is more upsetting than
       when it involves only others
    d. all of the above

15. Since people in Western cultures seem to accept the view that   *a*
    there should be a link between one's contributions and one's
    outcomes, the _____ is highly valued.
    a. equity rule   c. relative needs rule
    b. equality rule   d. desires rule

Multiple Choice Answers

1. a	(368)	9. d	(387)
2. d	(370)	10. a	(390)
3. b	(375)	11. a	(393)
4. c	(377)	12. b	(394)
5. b	(379)	13. c	(395)
6. c	(381)	14. d	(396)
7. a	(384)	15. a	(395)
8. b	(386)		

Just for Fun: Some Additional Readings

Lamb, M. Why Swedish fathers aren't liberated. Psychology Today,
    October, 1982. Sweden has enacted laws to benefit either
    mothers or fathers who choose to stay home with their children.
    Despite this "equality" under the law, equity in the marital
    dyad is still a long way off.

Hillix, W.A., Harari, H., and Mohr, D. Secrets. Psychology Today,
    September, 1979. What do people exchange in order to build
    intimacy? Secrets!

Rotter, J.B. Trust and gullibility. Psychology Today, October, 1980.
    Shows that high trusters are no less intelligent or more
    gullible than others. However, they are happier, more likable--
    and more trustworthy.

CHAPTER 11

GROUPS AND INDIVIDUAL BEHAVIOR: THE CONSEQUENCES OF BELONGING

Objectives

1. Summarize the "contradictory" findings of the early studies on the effect of presence of others on performance.

2. With regard to Zajonc's drive theory of social facilitation, summarize its assumptions, its predictions, and the research testing the predictions.

3. Compare the mere physical presence and evaluation apprehension hypotheses.

4. How does the distraction-conflict theory explain social facilitation effects? List its strengths and limitations.

5. Describe the social loafing effect and social impact theory. How can social loafing be reduced?

6. Describe the nature and consequences of deindividuation. How is it related to self-awareness?

7. Compare private and public self-awareness and specify the relationship of each to deindividuation.

8. What conclusions regarding deindividuation are supported by the Maruyama, Fraser, and Miller (1982) study?....by the Prentice-Dunn and Rogers (1982) study?

9. What suggestions are given for countering deindividuation?

10. Define the three social decision schemes, and note the circumstances under which each is used.

11. Summarize the findings of Kerr (1981) on social transition schemes.

12. What was the surprising finding of Stoner in his 1960s studies using choice-dilemma items?

13. Compare the risky shift and the shift toward polarization.

14. Discuss the process underlying group polarization according to the social comparison view. List supportive and contradictory findings.

15. Discuss the process underlying group polarization according to the persuasive arguments view. List supportive and contradictory findings.

16. Compare the great man/great woman and situational theories of leadership.

17. Contrast the "disappointing" early research findings with the more encouraging recent findings regarding the great man/great woman theory.

18. Describe the transactional perspective.

19. According to Fiedler's contingency model, what factors determine a leader's success?
    a) What two personal styles do leaders adopt?
    b) Under what situational conditions will each personal style be effective?
    c) What factors determine whether a situation is favorable or unfavorable to a leader?

Who Done It?

    Credit each of the concepts, theories, critical studies or important ideas listed below to the person or persons associated with each (e.g., item: Id-Ego-Superego; associated person: Freud). Answers are on the next page.

1. proposed drive theory of social facilitation *Zajonc*

2. proposed social impact theory *Latané et al*

3. proposed theory about nature of deindividuation *Diener*

4. modified Diener's theory (see above) to take into account two distinct types of self-awareness *Prentice-Dunn & Rogers*

5. study showing how social transition schemes work in decision-making "juries" *Kerr*

6. researcher who originally found "risky shift" *Stoner*

7. study of political leaders which finds encouraging results for great man/great woman theory of leadership *Constantine & Craik*

140

8. author of contingency model forpredicting leader effectiveness

Fiedler

Define

Each of the critical concepts listed below have been defined in your textbook. For each provide the definition. Answers are on the next page.

1. social facilitation : *the effect upon performance produced by the presence of others, either to improve or lower*
2. social loafing : *the greater the size of the group, the less effort each person puts out*
3. deindividuation : *the reduced concern over what others think and the lessened self awareness that occurs in various circumstances, often leading to impulsive forms of prohibited behavior*
4. social decision schemes : *rule that relate the initial distribution of member views to the groups final decision*
5. truth-wins rule : *the social decision schema that holds that a group will settle on the objectively correct decision*
6. polarization effect : *the intensification of attitude & opinions that occurs following group discussion.*
7. social comparision view of polarization : *the idea that we shift to more extreme positions in a group in order to reestablish our own self-image as a person holding desireable views*
8. persuasive arguments view of polarization : *the idea that we shift to more extreme positions in a group because the information that we are presented with is convincing*

Who Done It? Answers

1. Zajonc (414)
2. Latané and his colleagues (420)
3. Diener (424)
4. Prentice-Dunn and Rogers (424)
5. Kerr   (432)
6. Stoner (434)
7. Constantine and Craik (443)
8. Fiedler (444)

Matching

Match each concept or idea on the left with an identifying phrase, word or sentence on the right. Answers are on the next page.

A. diffusion of responsibility	F	1. predicted by social impact theory
B. enhances private self-awareness		
C. enhances public self-awareness	G	2. similar to contingency theory
D. first shift rule	B	3. "Focus on your own thoughts"
E. choice dilemma questions	C	4. "You'll meet your partner later"
F. social loafing effect		
G. transactional theory	E	5. used to measure risk-taking
H. drive theory prediction	D	6. momentum effect occurs
	H	7. audience increases arousal
	A	8. reduces helping in groups

Definitions

1. the effect upon performance produced by the presence of others; performance is sometimes improved and sometimes impaired (413)

2. the greater the size of the group, the less effort each person sometimes puts out (420)

3. the reduced concern over what others think and lessened self-awareness that occurs in various circumstances; it often produces impulsive forms of prohibited behavior (432)

4. rules that relate the initial distribution of member views to the group's final decision (429)

5. one of the social decision schemes; the idea is that the group will ultimately settle on an objectively correct decision (429)

6. the intensification of attitudes and opinions that occurs following group discussion (436)

7. we shift to more extreme positions in the group in order to re-establish our own self-image as a person holding desirable views (437)

8. we shift to more extreme positions in the group because the information presented by the other group members convinces us to change (437)

Matching Answers

1.	F (421)	5.	E (435)
2.	G (444)	6.	D (432)
3.	B (427)	7.	H (415)
4.	C (427)	8.	A (420)

Is Something Wrong Here?

For each statement below indicate what is wrong about the statement, if anything. If there _is_ something wrong, answer "yes" and indicate what's wrong. If nothing is wrong, answer "no; this one is correct." At the end of this exercise you will find the answers.

1. The term social facilitation, as the name suggests, refers only to situations where the presence of others leads to improvements in performance.

2. The fact that a blindfolded audience failed to produce a social facilitation effect in the Cottrell et al. experiment supports the "mere presence" hypothesis.

3. Performance of roaches is always better when it is carried out in the presence of other roaches. 142

correct

4. A crucial factor determining the size of the social loafing effect is the degree to which people think their individual performance can be monitored.

wrong

5. In the trick-or-treat study, deindividuation in ~~large~~ *small* groups was reduced by making each child responsible for his own donation of candy.

wrong

6. Aggression is facilitated by reductions in private self-awareness, ~~but not~~ *and* by reductions in public self-awareness.

correct

7. The social decisions scheme that seems to be the best at predicting the final group decision on judgmental tasks is the majority-wins rule.

wrong

8. The original studies by Stoner in the early 1960s comparing individual and group decisions found that groups made more conservative decisions than individuals.

correct *the other way around*

9. Current research concludes that when group members engage in discussion, the members typically show a polarization effect.

wrong

10. The text concludes that the persuasive arguments explanation for group polarization is correct and that the social comparison explanation is incorrect. *both views are correct*

wrong

11. Recent findings suggest that people high in need for power are likely to attain leadership ~~and~~ *but* to be successful when they do so. *unsuccessful*

correct

12. Fiedler's contingency model of leader effectiveness predicts that task-oriented leaders are more effective under highly unfavorable or highly favorable conditions, but that relations-oriented leaders are more effective under moderately favorable conditions.

Something Wrong Here? Answers

1. Yes; the term social facilitation can be misleading because it refers to <u>both</u> increases and decreases in performance. (415)

2. Yes; this finding supports the evaluation apprehension hypothesis. (417)

3. Yes; roaches show improved performance in the presence of other roaches when their dominant response is correct, but impaired performance when their dominant response is an error. (417)

4. No; this one is correct. (421)

5. Yes; making each child responsible did reduce deindividuation, but <u>only</u> in <u>small</u> groups. In large groups, deindividuation was "unstoppable." (426)

6. Yes; like other forms of unrestrained behavior, aggression is facilitated by a reduction in <u>both</u> types of self-awareness. (428)

7. No; this one is correct. (431)

8. Yes; groups made riskier decisions than individuals. (434)

9. No; this one is correct. (436)

10. Yes; both explanations are said to provide reasonably accurate accounts of polarization. (438)

11. Yes; these people are likely to become leaders, but they are typically not successful leaders. (442)

12. No; this one is correct. (445)

True-False

Indicate whether each of the following statements is true or false. Correct answers are at the end of the exercise.

F 1. Taken as a whole, the early studies concerned with the effects of the presence of others on performance indicated that the presence of others impaired performance.

F 2. In any given situation, the dominant response tendency is always the correct response.

F 3. The presence of others would be expected to improve performance in a situation where the person's dominant response is an error.

F 4. Social facilitation effects seem to occur only in the human species.

F 5. When students cheered as loudly as they could and could not be individually monitored, the amount of noise generated per person was greatest in the large groups.

F 6. Deindividuation is accompanied by increases in self-awareness.

T 7. Reductions in private self-awareness and reductions in public self-awareness both enhance the occurrence of impulsive, unrestrained behavior.

F 8. Reductions in private self-awareness and reductions in public self-awareness are both related to deindividuation.

F 9. Members of primitive societies do not seem to show deindividuation.

10. When people discuss their attitudes, the effect is usually to make them more moderate in their views.

11. The great man/great woman theory of leadership is strongly supported by the research findings.

12. On the basis of his contingency model of leader effectiveness, Fiedler has concluded that relations-oriented persons make better leaders.

True-False Answers

1. False; the early studies found that performance was sometimes improved and sometimes impaired by the presence of others. (414)

2. False; the dominant response tendency refers to the strongest response that the organism has in the situation, and it can be correct or incorrect. (416)

3. False; impaired performance is expected when an error tendency is dominant, improved performance when the dominant response is correct. (416)

4. False; social facilitation occurs in many species. (417)

5. False; people generated more noise when alone, i.e. there was "social loafing." (420)

6. False; Diener's theory says that deindividuation occurs when self-awareness is low. (425)

7. True   (424)

8. False; while both forms of self-awareness are related to impulsive behavior, only private self-awareness causes de-individuation. (424)

9. False; deindividuation occurs with a wide variety of subjects, including members of primitive societies. (426)

10. False; discussion generally causes people to become more extreme.
(436)

11. False; there has generally been little support for the theory, although recent findings are somewhat more encouraging. (440)

12. False; sometimes relations-oriented leaders are better, but sometimes task-oriented leaders are better. Which is better depends on the situation. (445)

Fill-in-the-Blanks

Complete the following statements by filling in the blanks with correct information. The answers are at the end of this exercise.

1. The area of research that studies the effect of the presence of others on an individual's performance is _social facilitation_ .

2. According to the _drive_ theory of social facilitation, the presence of others increases arousal, which in turn enhances the tendency to perform _dominant_ responses.

3. The _distraction - conflict_ hypothesis explains social facilitation results by assuming that the conflict between attending to the task vs. attending to the audience produces heightened motivation.

4. According to _social impact_ theory, the effect of any external force directed toward a group is divided between its members.

5. The term that refers to the lowered motivation that occurs when a person becomes convinced that his own contribution to the group is not essential is _the free rider effect_ .

6. The psychological state characterized by lessened self-awareness, reduced concern over social evaluation, and reduced restraints against prohibited forms of behavior is _deindividuation_ .

7. The text suggests three techniques for countering deindividuation. These techniques are: 1) _strengthening internal restraints_;
   2) _enhancing self-awareness_ and
   3) _countering anonymity_ .

8. Groups often seem to follow the _truth wins_ social decision scheme when an objectively correct decision exists.

9. The original studies by Stoner in the early 1960s found that groups shifted in the direction of advocating greater _risk_ following discussions of choice-dilemma questions.

10. According to the _social comparison_ theory of group polarization, we discover in group discussion that our views are more moderate than we had believed and shift to more extreme views in order to establish a more positive self-image.

11. The theory that leaders are distinguished from nonleaders by a small number of crucial traits is called the _great /man_ _great /woman_ theory by your text.

12. The _situational_ theory of leadership states that the person who can best help the group attain its goals because of some special competence will become the group leader.

13. The theory which views leadership as a reciprocal process of social influence where leaders influence followers and are, in turn, influenced by these persons is the _transactional_ theory.

Fill-in-the-Blank Answers

1. social facilitation (414)
2. drive; dominant (415)
3. distraction-conflict (418)
4. social impact (420)
5. the free-rider effect (422)
6. deindividuation (425)
7. strengthening internal restraints; enhancing self-awareness; countering anonymity (431)
8. truth-wins (432)
9. risk (434)
10. social comparison (437)
11. great man/great woman (439)
12. situational (440)
13. transactional (441)

Multiple Choice

d 1. The earliest experiments concerned with how the presence of others affects performance found that the presence of others
   a. had no significant effect on performance
   b. sometimes led to improved performance
   c. sometimes led to poorer performance
   d. both b and c were found

C 2. Research on the drive theory of social facilitation has found that
   a. the presence of others enhances the performance of dominant responses
   b. the presence of other persons is physiologically arousing
   c. both a and b
   d. neither a nor b

c 3. Which is <u>not</u> an assumption underlying the distraction-conflict explanation of social facilitation?
   a. organisms have a strong tendency to pay attention to the task at hand
   b. organisms have a strong tendency to pay attention to an audience
   c. the distraction produced by being in conflict causes the organisms to perform poorly
   d. the distraction produced by being in conflict leads to increases in the organisms' arousal

a 4. When Ringelmann measured the strength with which subjects pulled on a rope, he found that the force exerted per person was
   a. greatest when subjects were alone
   b. greatest when subjects were in small groups
   c. greatest when subjects were in larger groups
   d. greatest when subjects were in groups, regardless of size

a 5. When Latane, Williams, and Harkins (1979) asked male students to cheer as loudly as they could, the amount of noise generated by each person was greatest when the person was
   a. alone
   b. in a 2-person group
   c. in a 6-person group
   d. either b or c, since the number of coactors didn't matter

e 6. Which of the following contributes to the reduced effort and motivation shown by people in groups?
   a. free-rider effects
   b. social loafing
   c. the belief that other members are engaging in free-riding
   d. a and b
   e. a, b, and c

d 7. According to a theory proposed recently by Diener, the key factor in the occurrence of deindividuation is
   a. wild, impulsive behavior   c. feelings of anonymity
   b. increased arousal   d. blocking of self-awareness

148

d 8. In which settings has deindividuation been found to occur?
   a. research laboratories   c. public streets
   b. private homes   d. all of the above

a 9. Instructions given to subjects to focus their attention on their
   own thoughts and feelings while performing their tasks are designed to
   a. enhance private self-awareness c. reduce public self-awareness
   b. enhance public self-awareness   d. reduce private self-awareness

b 10. When the sheriff in a Hollywood western defuses an angry mob by
   calling individual members of the crowd by name, the tactic being
   used to counter deindividuation is
   a. enhancing self-awareness   c. strengthening internal restraints
   b. countering anonymity   d. social modeling

b 11. The idea that the group will ultimately adopt a position consistent with the direction of the first shift in opinion shown
   by any member is:
   a. the nonsense-wins rule   c. the social transition scheme
   b. the first-shift rule   d. the dominant member rule

d 12. Assume that a person wishes to influence the group decision. Which
   social decision scheme implies that she should start by supporting
   a view other than the one she actually favors and then change to
   the favored position?
   a. the majority-wins rule   c. the social transition scheme
   b. the truth-wins rule   d. the first-shift rule

c 13. When people discuss their views in a group with others who
   basically share their views
   a. their views become more moderate
   b. nobody changes since they already agree
   c. their views become more extreme
   d. the outcome of the discussion is impossible to predict

d 14. Support for the persuasive arguments explanation of group
   polarization is found in the fact that
   a. most of the arguments in a group discussion support the
      initially preferred view
   b. the greater the proportion of arguments favoring a particular
      view during a group discussion, the greater the shift in that
      direction
   c. most of the arguments in a group discussion support the
      initially nonpreferred view
   d. both a and b

b 15. If the trait theory of leadership were true, what practical
   benefit might result?
   a. we could train individuals to be highly effective leaders
   b. we could readily select those persons most qualified for
      leadership
   c. we would understand the roots of leadership in personality
   d. we could determine the situations in which a person would be
      an effective leader

16. In a recent study, Constantini and Craik (1980) compared the personality traits of political leaders to those of non-leaders. What did they find?
    a. political leaders did not differ from other persons in any important ways
    b. political leaders were actually lower than other persons on traits we would expect to be linked to leadership (e.g., dominance, self-confidence)
    c. political leaders were less intelligent and less honest than other persons
    d. political leaders were higher on some traits and lower on others than "average" persons

17. Fiedler's contingency model of leadership
    a. views leadership as a complex social relationship, in which leaders both influence and are influenced by their followers
    b. holds that leaders rise to positions of authority because they possess special traits
    c. states that the leader's orientation and the favorability of the situation interact to determine leader effectiveness
    d. emphasizes the importance of situational factors in determining leader effectiveness

Multiple Choice Answers

1. d (414)	10. b (430)
2. c (416)	11. b (430)
3. c (418)	12. d (432)
4. a (420)	13. c (436)
5. a (420)	14. d (438)
6. e (422)	15. b (440)
7. d (424)	16. d (442)
8. d (426)	17. c (444)
9. a (427)	

<u>Just for Fun: Some Additional Readings</u>

Janis, Irving L. Groupthink. <u>Psychology Today</u>, November, 1971.
    Various high-level governmental decisions are analyzed in terms
    of "groupthink"--"a deterioration of mental efficiency, reality
    testing and moral judgment that results from ingroup pressures."

Colligan, M.J., and Stockton, W. The mystery of assembly-line
    hysteria. <u>Psychology Today</u>, June, 1978. The interesting group
    phenomenon of mass psychogenic illness in industrial settings is
    discussed.

Harder, Mary W., Richardson, James T. and Simonds, Robert B. Jesus
    people. <u>Psychology Today</u>, December, 1972. This article deals
    with explanations for the dramatic behavior changes often found
    among "Jesus people." Rather than accept the explanation that
    they've "found Christ," the authors interpret the changes in
    terms of group dynamcis.

CHAPTER 12

ENVIRONMENT AND BEHAVIOR

Objectives

1. Define "environmental psychology" and "personal space." Tell how the latter varies around the world, between adults and children, among same and different sexed strangers, among people differing in socio-economic class, and among violent and nonviolent individuals.

2. Define "proxemics," "intimate distance," "social distance," and "public distance." Indicate the nature of "distance," the distance most prefer in general, the distance to a friend that is preferred, and the general affect of closeness.

3. Describe the typical findings with regard to invasions of personal space. What happens when the invasion is via camera? What determines whether an invasion results in anger, fear or being pleased.

4. What are the ins and outs of being an invader (pay attention to the water fountain studies)? What about coming between people who are conversing and who vary by sex and race?

5. Define "territory," "territoriality," "primary territory," "secondary territory" and "public territory." Where do people feel most comfortable in general and at home? What are "markers" used for? With regard to territoriality, what determines who is likely to stay in school? Describe the prior residence effect, or home team advantage, and its influence on behavior.

6. Describe the variations in what happens when a crowd gathers to watch a person who is perched on a high ledge, threatening suicide. Define "contagion." Tell how Mann (1981) chose to study the type of suicide described above. Discuss the circumstances, including deindividuation, that determines how a crowd will react to a "person on a ledge."

153

7. Describe the now classic "crowded rats" studies by Calhoun.
    Discuss how crowding (sheer numbers of people) influences a
    variety of behaviors, from divorce to voting. Indicate the
    difference between density and crowding. How do people react
    to the feeling of being crowded and what's the difference
    between social and spatial density?

8. Indicate what factors determine whether exposure to density
    leads to negative or positive feelings and reactions, including
    in the dorms. Discuss the influences of personality factors
    on reactions to density.

9. What single factor seems to account for the unpleasant effects
    of crowding? Discuss the diverse factors that can lessen the
    negative impact of crowding, including everything from close-
    ness to elevator control panels, placement of tents at a camp-
    site to signs in the hallways of a prison.

loss of control

10. What is "stress"? Define the terms of Lazarus and Cohen's
    (1977) classification of stressful events. What is the range of
    reactions to stress? What determines the impact of noise on
    behavior and how does noise relate to health? Indicate how
    children who attend schools near airports react to the constant
    noise and how noise influences violence.

11. Describe how heat influences performance, and the curvilinear
    relationship between heat and aggression, as well as exceptions
    to the latter. Describe the incidence of air pollution in this
    country and elsewhere. How does foul air influence health,
    including automobile fumes and cigarette smoke? How does
    dirty air influence behavior?

12. Indicate where people like to live, including the influence of
    "what you're used to." What factors may play a role in deciding
    on an ideal site, and to what locations are people migrating?
    Discuss the preference for "savannas."

13. Describe the "population shift." Name the two factors hat
    determine emotional response to a surrounding. Indicate the
    kind of setting that people describe as positive and the kind
    they see as negative. List the variety of behaviors that are
    influenced by the excitement of the city.

14. Describe the ideal environments created by James Rouse and
    restoration efforts around the country.

15. What are the two horns of the over-population dilemma? Discuss
    the rate of increase of population in the U.S. A billion people
    could fill how many Chicagos 308 and how rapidly does a billion
    people expand? What is the logical outcome of endless popula-
    tion explosion? What are the alternative solutions to the
    population explosion?

154

Who Done It?

Credit each of the concepts, theories, critical studies or important ideas listed below to the person or persons associated with each (e.g., item: Id-Ego-Superego; associated person: Freud). The correct answers are on the next page.

1. derived the four basic interpersonal distances *Hall*

2. did one of the first "invasion of personal space" studies *Felipe & Sommer*

3. did the study of crowds gathering at the scene of a "suicide by jump" *Mann*

4. curvilinear relationship between heat and aggression *Baron*

5. devised terms for classification of stressful events *Lazarus & Cohen*

6. created ideal environments *Rouse*

7. did the famous "crowded rat" studies *Calhoun*

Define

Each of the critical concepts listed below have been defined in your textbook. For each provide the definition. Answers are on the next page.

1. environmental psychology: *deals with the interaction between the physical world & human behavior*

2. personal space: *the zone around each individual into which most other people are not supposed to trespass / an extension of themselves*

3. territoriality: *a variety of actions which people engage in to stake out and protect portions of their environment from intrusion*

4. public territory: *a space that is occupied only temporarily, & which is available to other; ie) park bench*

5. proxemics: *the study of the distance people place between and among themselves in various kinds of interactions*

6. spatial density: *the size of the place occupied by a given number of individuals*

7. social density: *the number of persons who occupy a space of a given one*

8. state of density: *the objective physical condition defined by the number of people occupying a particular space of a given size*

9. state of crowding: *the psychological state of feeling that too many people occupy a space; causes stress*

155

Who Done It Answers

1. Hall (457)
2. Felipe and Sommer (459)
3. Mann (466)
4. Baron (474)

5. Lazarus and Cohen (470)
6. Rouse (480)
7. Calhoun (465)

Definitions

1. is a relatively new field of study that deals with the interaction between the physical world and human behavior (454)

2. the area immediately around persons' bodies that they regard as an extension of themselves (455)

3. manifested in staking out and defending of space against members of one's own species (461)

4. an area that is temporarily possessed by whoever gets there first (461)

5. the study of the distances at which Americans interact (457)

6. refers to a constant number of people occupying spaces of varying sizes (468)

7. refers to a constant physical space being occupied by varying numbers of people (468)

8. refers to the objective physical state of many people occupying the same space (465)

9. refers to the psychological state of feeling that too many people occupy a space (465)

Matching

On the next page you will find the matching exercise. Match each concept or idea on the left with an identifying phrase, word or sentence on the right by drawing a line from concept to phrase. The correct answers for the matching questions are on the bottom of the page; cover them with a piece of paper.

156

A. relief of crowding and stress
B. Americans
C. savannas
D. contagion
E. public distance
F. erectors of fenses, signs and hedges
G. homeowners with markers on their property
H. children chronically exposed to airplane noise
I. resort to cannibalism when over-crowded
J. females

_D_ 1. the spread of a behavior throughout a crowd
_E_ 2. greatest distance at which people interact
_H_ 3. give up on completion of a task
_B_ 4. people who prefer greater interpersonal distances than Greeks, French, and Arabs
_A_ 5. division of dorms into smaller units
_F_ 6. people who rush to the door when the bell rings
_C_ 7. flat, grassy plains with a scattering of trees
_J_ 8. people for whom density is generally positive
_I_ 9. rats
_G_ 10. people who are relatively fearless about crime

Is Something Wrong Here?

For each statement below indicate what is incorrect about the statement if anything. If there is something wrong, answer "yes" and indicate what's wrong. If nothing is wrong, answer "no; this one is correct." At the end of this exercise you will find the answers.

correct
1. It might be helpful to think of closeness as something that varies along a continuum and not as a series of mysterious regions that differ in their effects.

wrong
2. Invaders of personal spaces are ~~always~~ *often* unwelcome.

wrong
3. While passing two people who are conversing in a hallway, be sure to pass between them only if they are standing ~~close to~~ *far from* one another.

correct
4. When one sits down in a public area, such as a public library, one may feel helpless to control violations of her/his personal space.

correct

5. Individuals are more likely to pass between people who are conversing if they are black than if they are white.

wrong

6. Noise is bad enough, but when it is present ~~constantly~~, *intermittently* it has its most harmful effects.

wrong   *decreases*

7. Noise ~~increases~~ helping because it makes potential helpers feel badly ~~and they help to restore good feelings.~~

wrong

8. The population shift in the U.S. has been basically westward. *↓ south*

wrong

9. In Seattle, manhole covers are being redesigned to depict ~~country scenes.~~ *maps of the city*

correct

10. The kinds of environments to which people react positively have trees, grass and bodies of water.

correct

11. The excitement of the city is manifested in the fact that people walk faster.

correct

12. Emotional reactions to surroundings fall along two dimensions, excitement and pleasantness.

wrong

13. "Prior resident effect" is another name for "possession is nine-tenths of the law." *the home field advantage*

correct

14. People whose privacy is invaded via camera tend to flee.

wrong

15. "~~Intimate~~ distance" is used for conversations with friends. *Personal*

Is Something Wrong Here? Answers

1. No; this one is correct. (457)

2. Yes; friends and especially attractive members of the opposite sex may be welcomed with open arms. (459)

3. Well, you could do this, but if you do, you will be violating hallway etiquette. (460)

4. No; this one is correct. (450)

5. No; this one is correct. (460)

6. Yes; intermittent or variable noise generates the most harmful effects. (471)

7. Yes; noise lowers the likelihood of helping. (472)

8. Yes; this is so, with the exception of Florida. (478)

9. Yes; covers depict maps to help pedestrians. (481)

10. No; this one is correct. (479)

11. No; this one is correct. (479)

12. No; this one is correct. (477)

13. Yes; it is "home field advantage." (463)

14. No; this one is correct. (459)

15. Yes; it is "personal distance." (457)

True-False

Indicate whether each of the following statements is true or false. Correct answers are at the end of this exercise.

F 1. Violent individuals have small personal space.

F 2. In the lavatory study of interpersonal distancing at the urinal, the nearer the collaborator was to the subject, the less time it took the subject to begin urinating.

T 3. A territory is different from a personal space in that the former is a stationary bounded area that regulates who may enter.

F 4. Altman's (1975) three types of human territories are singletary, secondary, and tertiary.

T 5. If it is possible to predict the presentation of noise, its aversive effects are much diminished.

T 6. In general, high heat levels tend to lower performance.

F 7. Crowding influences a whole host of common behaviors, except voting and divorce.

T 8. Chronic noise can increase the incidence of strokes and birth defects.

T 9. Airborne chemicals can cause skin and lung cancer.

F 10. According to Rotten et al. (1978), subjects in a polluted atmosphere finished a task less quickly than those in a normal atmosphere.

T 11. A billion people could inhabit 308 cities the size of Chicago.

F 12. Contributing to the "over-population dilemma" is (1) our planet has an over abundance of resources and (2) human reproduction is steadily decreasing.

T 13. It is difficult to generalize about "where people like to live," because humans seem able to adapt to just about any environment.

F 14. In one study, freshmen who left school were more likely to decorate their rooms with diverse items and with maps and photos of the university region.

True-False Answers

1. False; they have large personal spaces. (456)

2. False; the more time it took to begin urinating. (458)

3. True. (461)

4. Mainly false; these are primary, secondary, and public. (461)

5. True. (451)

6. True. (473)

7. False; voting and divorce are also influenced. (461)

8. True. (471)

9. True. (475)

10. False; they finished more quickly, supposedly to get the heck out of there. (476)

11. True. (484)

12. False; it is lack of resources and increasing reproduction. (482)

13. True. (478)

14. False; it was those who stay. (462)

Fill in the Blanks

Complete the statements on the next page by filling in the blanks with correct information. The answers are at the end of this exercise.

1. With increase in age of children there is an increase in the
    _____distance_____ maintained between participants in inter-
    personal interactions.

2. Being forced by circumstances to invade someone else's
    _____personal space_____ is nearly always unpleasant for the
    invader.

3. Feelings of _____helplessness_____ accompany lack of control over
    one's environment.

4. In general, the U.S. population is located in the _____urban areas_____.

5. According to Edney (1975 study of visiting others in their dorm
    rooms) the "prior resident effect" is something like what sports
    announcers often refer to as the _____home field advantage_____.

6. Thousands of years from now the logical outcome of an ever
    increasing population will be a universe composed of
    _____human flesh_____.

7. In the home, public places include _____bathroom_____,
    _____hallways_____ and _____living rooms_____.

8. Variable noise is so aversive because it is so _____unpredictable_____.

9. Loss of hearing, birth defects and even death are among the
    physical effects of prolonged exposure to _____noise_____.

10. The _____labeling_____ of physiological _____arousal_____
    determines whether invasion will be accompanied by fear, anger
    or pleasure.

11. The presence of a stranger near a water fountain has _____not_____
    _____ affect on drinking behavior in a densely packed
    hallway.

12. At parties crowding can have positive effects. In college
    dorms crowding has _negative_ effects.

13. People from lower socio-economic levels tend to interact more
    closely than their upper-level counterparts.

14. Over _half_ of U.S. citizens live in cities where
    the air is seriously polluted.

Fill-in-the-Blank Answers

 1. distance (455)
 2. personal space (460)
 3. helplessness (470)
 4. urban areas (or cities) (476)
 5. "home field advantage" (464)
 6. human flesh (484)
 7. bathrooms, living rooms and hallways (462)
 8. unpredictable (471)
 9. noise (471)
10. labeling; arousal (459)
11. no   (460)
12. negative (469)
13. closely (456)
14. half   (475)

Multiple Choice

1. "Environmental psychology" is
   - a. an application of psychological theory to the study of environmental problems such as pollution
   - b. a relatively new field of study that deals with the relationship between a physical world and human behavior
   - c. the application of ecological theory in biology to the study of human behavior
   - d. the study of how people's behavior influences trends in weather

2. According to Hall, the study of the spacing between individuals is called
   - a. environmental psychology
   - b. personal spacology
   - c. proxemics
   - d. bubble psychology

3. Which of the following are among Hall's four interpersonal distances for Americans?
   - a. sexual
   - b. personal
   - c. private
   - d. all of the above

4. What happened when a stranger pointed a camera at passers-by?
   - a. most reacted submissively such as running
   - b. most physically attacked the man with the camera
   - c. most verbally attacked the man with the camera
   - d. both d and c

5. The presence of a stranger near a water fountain has no influence on attempts to drink when
   - a. there are few people around
   - b. the stranger is the only person present
   - c. the area is densely packed
   - d. all involved are elderly

6. Which of the following is used regularly, but is shared with others?
   - a. primary territory
   - c. public territory
   - c. private territory
   - d. secondary territory

7. Which of the following is an example of a frequently used "marker" for staking out territory?
   - a. coat
   - b. blank piece of paper
   - c. pencil on a desk
   - d. all of the above

8. In Edney's (1975) study, where did Yale undergraduates function the most effectively?
   - a. on neutral territory
   - b. their own dormitory room
   - c. someone else's dormitory room
   - d. in a wide open space

163

9. When Calhoun in his famous "crowded rat" studies placed rats in a roomy housing apparatus and just allowed them to breed freely, what kinds of behaviors increased as over-population increased?
   a. altruistic behaviors
   b. inappropriate sex role behavior: male rats began to show maternal behavior
   c. cannibalism
   d. a lowered level of sexual behavior

10. Density can lead to negative feelings when
    a. others present are having fun
    b. crowding conditions lead to goal blockage
    c. one has joined the crowd voluntarily
    d. the temperature is moderate

11. What probably accounts for the negative feelings that accompany crowding?
    a. being too close to persons of the same sex
    b. loss of control
    c. restriction of freedom of movement
    d. lowering the number of behavioral options

12. Which of the following kinds of noise is the most aversive?
    a. steady, constant noise
    b. noise that occurs intermittently and therefore is unpredictable
    c. low frequency noise (10 cycles per second or lower)
    d. mechanical noise

13. When Bell (1978b) increased temperature and noise level, how was performance influenced?
    a. surprisingly temperature raised performance level, and noise left it uneffected
    b. surprisingly temperature lowered performance level, but noise raised it
    c. both temperature and noise elevations lowered performance level
    d. surprisingly neither noise or temperature influenced performance level

14. What is the incidence of air pollution in this country and elsewhere?
    a. over half of the U.S. population lives in cities with polluted air
    b. almost one third of the U.S. populative lives in areas that are seriously polluted
    c. air pollution is worse in the U.S. than in other countries
    d. both a and c

15. The preference for savannas shown by children may be
    a. due to the simplicity of the setting
    b. learned from watching the movies
    c. inborn
    d. due to imitation of adults

164

16. Reactions to the excitement of the city include
    a. establishing eye contact with others
    c b. seeking the "outstretched hand"
    c. walking faster
    d. all of the above

17. One billion people would fill up _____ cities the size of
    Chicago.
    b a. 100   c. 55
        b. 308   d. 505

Multiple Choice Answers

1. b (454)		10. b (469)	
2. c (457)		11. b (470)	
3. b (457)		12. b (471)	
4. a (458)		13. c (473)	
5. c (460)		14. a (475)	
6. d (461)		15. c (479)	
7. a (462)		16. c (479)	
8. b (464)		17. b (484)	
9. c (465)			

Just for Fun: Some Additional Readings

Rubin, Z.   Seasonal rhythms in behavior. Psychology Today, December, 1979. When the sun shines, so do the people. When the rain falls, so do the spirits of the people. You've always suspected as much, but psychologists are just now beginning to investigate how we change when the weather changes.

Senders, J.W.   Is there a cure for human error? Psychology Today. April, 1980. "Then he pulls another switch, though he can't remember which is the proper one to turn on at this point. So the core is running loose and the radioactive juice is now starting to appear at every point." JWS. Is it possible to prevent the kind of human error that ends in environmental disaster? Yes, by a better mesh of "man" and machine.

Waters, H.   Life according to TV. Newsweek, December 6, 1982. Besides promoting violence, TV does little else to behavior, right? Wrong. Recent research indicates that TV shapes--in fact, distorts--our reality to a significant degree.

Raloff, J.   Noise cna be hazardous to our health. Science News, June 5, 1982. Noise is a great deal more than a nuisance. It's a killer.

CHAPTER 13

APPLYING SOCIAL PSYCHOLOGY

Objectives

1. Define applied social psychology and forensic psychology.

2. Summarize the research on accuracy of eyewitness testimony.

3. Describe how the following aspects of the attorneys' behavior affect the trial outcome:
   a) Opening statement.
   b) Photos/words used.
   c) Adversary vs. nonadversary arrangement.

4. How are jurors affected by the judge's instructions to disregard certain testimony and by the judge's final instructions?

5. Summarize the effects that the behavior, appearance, and attitudes of defendants have on jurors.

6. Indicate how the traits and attitudes of jurors influence their decisions.

7. Describe the evaluation research done with the neighborhood crime project in Hartford.

8. How is the practice of effective preventive behavior related to personality?

9. Describe the smoking-prevention program used with children and teenagers.

10. Summarize the effects of stress on health.
    a) How does perceived control influence our reaction to stress?
    b) How can the effects of stress be reduced?

11. What interpersonal variables influence the interaction between patient and medical specialist?

12. Summarize the effects produced by hospital and nursing home environments.

13. Note the techniques used to initiate environmental improvements on problems of pollution, littering, energy use, ride-sharing, and surroundings.

14. How is the worker viewed from the vantage point of scientific management theory, the human relations approach, and the "work ethic"?

15. What factors determine job satisfaction?

16. Summarize the negative effects that occur when circadian processes are disrupted.

17. How do attribution processes affect the evaluation that is made of one's job performance?

Who Done It?

Credit each of the concepts, theories, critical studies or important ideas listed below to the person or persons associated with each (e.g., item: Id-Ego-Superego; associated person: Freud). Answers are on the next page.

1. study showing that the overwhelming majority of subjects were no better than chance at eyewitness identification
   Buckout

2. study showing that words used in question ("bump" vs. "smash") affects how subjects answer
   Loftus

3. study showing that unattractive defendants were more likely to be imprisoned than attractive ones
   Stewart

4. study comparing response of authoriatrian and egalitarian jurors to citizen vs. policeman *Mitchell*

5. devised smoking prevention program for youths
   Evans

6. data showing that lower socioeconomic status patients remembered more of the information provided by physicians
   Pendleton

7. study showing that littering behavior depends on presence of existing litter and reminder signs
   Reiter & Samuel

168

Who Done It? Answers

1. Buckout (493)
2. Loftus (495)
3. Stewart (499)
4. Mitchell (501)
5. Evans (506)
6. Pendleton (512)
7. Reiter and Samuel (517)

Define

Each of the critical concepts listed below have been defined in your textbook. For each provide the definition. Answers are on the next page.

1. application: the use of research findings to solve practical, everyday problems
2. forensic psychology: the study of the relationship between psychology and the law
3. authoritarianism: the personality dimension that ranges from the authoritarian personality to the egalitarian personality
4. evaluation research: research designed to determine the effect of any program of social intervention in terms of costs, benefit, or impact upon individuals
5. behavioral medicine: research & application with regards to the psychological factors in the prevention and treatment of physical illness
6. perceived control: the degree to which an individual believes that he/she is in control of the events of his/her life
7. organizational behavior: the field that studies human behavior in organizational settings
8. circadian processes: any bodily process that occurs in a 24-hour cycle

Matching

Match each concept or idea on the left with an identifying phrase, word or sentence on the right. Answers are on the next page.

A. Stockholm syndrome
B. photo of goldenrod plants
C. informed patients
D. flexitime
E. egalitarianism
F. chronic depression
G. attractive swindler
H. same-race defendant

H 1. believed in rape-trial study
D 2. reduces absenteeism
G 3. judged harshly
A 4. close bonds with captors
F 5. related to low sense of control
B 6. can induce sneezing
C 7. pain is made more bearable
E 8. opposite of authoritarianism

169

Definitions

1. the use of research findings to solve practical, everyday problems (490)

2. the study of psychological factors that influence the legal process (492)

3. cluster of personality characteristics that includes submission to authority, rigid conformity to social norms, and hostile rejection of persons who deviate from norms (500)

4. research designed to determine the effects of a social intervention program; costs, benefits, and impact of the program are measured (502)

5. research and application with regard to the effects of psychological factors in the prevention and treatment of physical illness (504)

6. the degree to which a person believes that he/she is able to affect the course of events in his/her own life (509)

7. the field that studies human behavior in organizational settings (514)

8. any bodily process that occurs in a 24-hour cycle (520)

Matching Answers

1. H (500) 5. F (509)
2. D (518) 6. B (504)
3. G (499) 7. C (513)
4. A (502) 8. E (500)

Is Something Wrong Here?

For each statement below indicate what is wrong about the statement, if anything. If there is something wrong, answer "yes" and indicate what's wrong. If nothing is wrong, anwer "no; this one is correct." At the end of this exercise you will find the answers.

correct

1. According to Salazar (1981), the primary activity of social psychologists in third world countries should be application.

wrong

2. The percentage of new Ph.D.s who have accepted jobs in universities over the past few years has increased from about one-third to about one-half of the group. *decreased*

wrong half   third

3. In Buckout's (1980) study of eyewitness identification, most of the subjects correctly identified the "criminal."

incorrectly

4. Subjects told that an eyewitness was without his needed eyeglasses when the crime occurred simply ignored the discredited testimony. *wrong* *The found defendant guilty*

5. Lengthy opening statements seem to bore the jurors and thus produce less impact on the final verdict. *wrong* *they have greater impact*

6. The use of color slides of a victim's injury led to the jury awarding less money in damages than when the same injury was simply described verbally. *wrong* *more*

7. Attractive defendants are generally treated more leniently than relatively unattractive defendants. *correct*

8. The biggest obstacle in getting people to act in their own best interests so as to prevent medical problems is their lack of knowledge about what to do. *wrong* *motivation to follow a plan*

9. There is data indicating that an increase in unemployment is followed by an increased death rate due to stress-related diseases. *correct*

10. When children are told what a dentist is doing and what to expect, they report less anxiety and less physical discomfort. *correct*

11. Two-thirds of Americans say they would quit work if they had enough money to buy whatever they wanted. *wrong* *keep using over*

12. There is no relationship between a person's job satisfaction and how often the person is absent from work. *wrong*

13. People adapt to jet lag more readily after eastbound travel than after westbound travel. *wrong* *west* *east*

14. In evaluating performance, evaluators seem to pay more attention to effort than to ability. *correct*

Is Something Wrong Here? Answers

1. No; this one is correct. (490)

2. Yes; the percentage hired by universities has <u>decreased</u>. (490)

3. Yes; the number of correct identifications was very low; in fact near chance. (493)

4. Yes; these subjects decided the defendant was <u>guilty</u>, despite the discrediting of the testimony. (494)

5. Yes; lengthy statements have <u>greater</u> impact. (495)

6. Yes; the result was just the opposite, clear slides led the jury to aware <u>more</u> money. (495)

7. No; this one is correct. (499)

8. Yes; the biggest obstacle is their lack of motivation to follow a program. (505)

9. No; this one is correct. (508)

10. No; this one is correct. (511)

11. Yes; two-thirds say they would <u>continue</u> to work under this circumstance. (518)

12. Yes; in fact, satisfied employees are absent from work less often. (519)

13. Yes; just the opposite is true. (522)

14. No; this one is correct. (523)

True-False

Indicate whether each of the following statements is true or false. Correct answers are at the end of the exercise.

T 1. Children are relatively accurate as eyewitnesses.

T 2. Discussion among witnesses before testimony has been found to increase the accuracy of testimony.

F 3. When eyewitnesses are encouraged to make guesses, and not allowed to say, "I don't know," their accuracy increases.

T 4. The sex, race, socioeconomic status, and appearance of the witness have all been shown to play a role in determining what verdict is reached.

F 5. How the question was phrased to subjects in the Loftus (1980) study did not affect their perception of the auto accident.

F 6. The least satisfied defendants in a court case seem to be those who take part in a nonadversarial procedure and lose.

F 7. Serving in a trial in which the prosecution makes a strong case leads to greater punitiveness in a subsequent trial.

F 8. There has been an increased tendency to be lenient with rapists over the past decade.

9. The evaluation research done on the Hartford crime control project found that the frequency of crime was not reduced although peoples' _fear_ of crime was reduced.

10. The smoking program devised by Evans and his associates deals with teen-age smoking by giving smokers drugs that make them nauseous when they smoke.

11. Rodin and Janis (1979) suggest that the way for a physician to build a relationship with a patient is for the physician to establish his authority over the patient.

12. Patients are more likely to start a conversation with a nurse dressed in a standard white uniform than with a nurse dressed in street clothes.

13. Research with hospitalized patients suggests that the more they know about the medical procedures they will undergo, the more frightening the procedures are.

14. There seems to be no way in which memory loss in the elderly can be reversed.

True-False Answers

1. True (494)

2. True (494)

3. False; these conditions decrease accuracy. (494)

4. True (494)

5. False; simply changing from the word "bumped" to the word "smashed" increased the frequency of broken glass being "seen." (495)

6. False; least satisfied are those who lose after taking part in an _adversarial_ procedure. (496)

7. False; "jurors" showed greater leniency in the second trial. (501)

8. False; just the opposite! (502)

9. False; frequency of crime was reduced, along with fear of burglary. (502)

10. False; Evans tries to convince people to never start smoking in the first place. (506)

11. False; the physician should establish similarities between self and patient and should express a positive evlaution of the patient. (512)

173

12. False; they are more likely to interact with the nurse dressed in street clothes. (512)

13. False; in fact, patients react better to treatment the more they know about the medical procedures. (513)

14. False; loss can be reversed if elderly patients are encouraged to engage in cognitive activity and are rewarded for doing so. (513)

Fill-in-the-Blanks

Complete the following statements by filling in the blanks with correct information. The answers are at the end of this exercise.

1. The specialty of ___forensic___ psychology studies the relationship between psychology and the law.

2. Witnesses interviewed by a ___nonadversary___ lawyer gave more accurate accounts of the tape-recorded bar fight.

3. Minor crimes committed while drinking drew ___less___ severe sentences than the same crimes committed while sober.

4. In the Segall and Ostrove (1975) experiment, jurors were more lenient when judging an ___attractive___ ~~swindl~~ burglar.

5. The personality trait that includes submission to authority, conformity to conventional norms, and hostility toward persons who violate these norms is ___authoritarianism___.

6. The study by Mitchell (1979) found that egalitarians were fair when the defendant was a ___citizen___, and authoritarians were fair when the defendant was a ___policeman___.

7. Research which tries to determine the effects of a new program by measuring its costs, its benefits, and its impact on individuals is called ___evaluation___ research.

8. One thing than cannot be determined by evaluation research is what the ___goals___ of the program should be.

174

9. While cigarette smoking is declining among most groups in the U.S. population, it is increasing among _young females_ .

10. An important factor in how one responds to electric shock, loud noise, old age, retirement, relocation, etc. is one's ___sense of control___ .

11. Physicians seem to provide the ___least___ information to working-class patients, while low socioeconomic status patients seem to remember ___more___ of the information than higher status patients.

12. The ___scientific management___ approach to management and organizational behavior emphasizes the importance of designing jobs and tasks efficiently and of monetary incentives to motivate workers.

13. The ___human relations___ approach to management and organizational behavior is compatible with the finding that personal satisfaction from a job is more important than financial satisfaction.

14. The belief that work makes someone a better person is called ___the work ethic___ .

15. Designing jobs so as to increase the number and variety of tasks performed by each worker is called ___job enlargement___ .

16. Blue-collar workers find more job satisfaction in the ___public___ sector, and white-collar workers find more job satisfaction in the ___private___ sector.

17. The term that refers to the individual's feelings of loyalty to the organization for which he/she works, and to the level of identification and involvement with it, is ___job commitment___ .

18. Daily cycles in biological functioning follow the "_circadian_" principle.

19. Supervisors give ___more___ credit than is due for a good performance and ___more___ blame than is due for a bad performance.

Fill-in-the-Blank Answers

1. forensic (492)
2. nonadversary (496)
3. less (498)
4. attractive (499)
5. authoritarianism (500)
6. citizen; policeman (501)
7. evaluation (502)
8. goals (503)
9. young females (506)
10. sense of control (510)
11. least; more (512)
12. scientific management (515)
13. human relations (515)
14. the work ethic (515)
15. job enlargement (518)
16. public; private (518)
17. job commitment (519)
18. circadian (520)
19. more; more (522)

Multiple Choice

1. "Social-psychological research and practice in real-world settings directed toward the understanding of human social behavior and the attempted solution of social problems" This is a definition of
   a. forensic psychology
   b. organizational psychology
   c. evaluation research
   d. applied social psychology

2. In one study drug-store clerks were asked to identify two customers who had been in their store in the past two hours. How often were the clerks able to accurately identify the customers?
   a. virtually all the time
   b. 75% of the time
   c. 33% of the time
   d. virtually never

3. Loftus (1974) demonstrated to subjects that the one eyewitness to a crime needed eyeglasses but was without them when the crime occurred. When these subjects formed a jury to decide the defendant's fate on the basis of the nearsighted person's testimony, the jury
   a. decided that the defendant was guilty
   b. ignored the discredited witness's testimony
   c. decided that the defendant was not guilty
   d. both b and c

4. To maximize their impact on the jury, the prosecution or defense should present a _____ opening statement and _____ promise to present evidence later on that will be overwhelmingly convincing.
   a. brief; should
   b. brief; should not
   c. lengthy; should
   d. lengthy; should not

5. Defendants in a court case seem to be the least satisfied when they take part in
   a. a nonadversarial procedure and lose
   b. an adversarial procedure and lose
   c. a and b are equally frustrating
   d. an adversarial procedure, whether they win or lose
   e. a nonadversarial procedure, whether they win or lose

6. Minor crimes committed while drinking drew _____ severe sentences than the same crimes committed while sober; serious crimes committed while drinking drew _____ severe sentences.
   a. less; less
   b. more; more
   c. less; more
   d. more; less

7. For which has the race of the defendant been shown to play a role?
   a. the believability of a rape trial defendant
   b. the percentage of defendants convicted in actual criminal trials
   c. whether an actual defendnat is imprisoned or not
   d. all of the above
   e. b and c

177

8. The study by Mitchell (1979) found that egalitarians were fair when the defendant was _____, and that authoritarians were _____.

   d
   a. a policeman; never fair
   b. a citizen; never fair
   c. a policeman; fair when the defendant was a citizen
   d. a citizen; fair when the defendant was a policeman

9. Which was not part of the Hartford crime control project?

   d
   a. a police team was assigned permanently to the neighborhood
   b. resident organizations were formed
   c. some aspects of the neighborhood environment were redesigned
   d. residents were encouraged to purchase guns as a deterrent to criminals

10. Statement A. The belief that illness is a purely physical problem which requires physical means of prevention and cure is more firmly held now than ever before in history.
    Statement B. The involvement of psychologists in the field of behavioral medicine has declined in recent years.

    b
    a. both statements are true
    b. both statements are false
    c. statement A is true; statement B is false
    d. statement B is true; statement A is false

11. The smoking prevention program devised by Evans and his associates to deal with teenage smoking

    c
    a. uses drugs that make smokers nauseous
    b. relies on scare tactics to frighten potential smokers
    c. tries to convince people to never start smoking
    d. focuses on those who already smoke
    e. both a and d

12. What is the conclusion reached by Hendrick et al. (1982) regarding the effects of old age, retirement, and relocation on stress?

    b
    a. the factors are inherently stressful
    b. the factors are not stressful so long as the person maintains a sense of control
    c. the factors are stressful only when one allows himself to seek the helpful support of others
    d. the factors are stressful only when one allows himself to accept his feelings as being perfectly legitimate

13. Sterling (1980) found that _____ patients are _____ likely to interact with a nurse dressed in a standard white uniform than with a nurse in street clothes.

    e
    a. male; more
    b. female; more
    c. male; less
    d. female; less
    e. both c and d

14. Which statement is true?
    a. nursing home patients given greater responsibility for them-
       selves show an increased mortality rate
    b. the most adaptive way for nursing home patients to respond to
       their environment is to be apathetic
    c. nursing home patients given plants to care for simply allow
       them to die
    d. memory loss in the elderly can be reversed if they are
       encouraged to engage in cognitive activity and are rewarded for
       doing so

15. _____ is the field that seeks to understand and predict
    human behavior in organizational settings by studying individuals,
    groups, and the structure and function of organizations.
    a. forensic psychology   c. applied social psychology
    b. organizational behavior   d. evaluation research

Multiple Choice Answers

1. d (490)   9. d (502)
2. c (494) 10. b (504)
3. a (494) 11. c (506)
4. c (495) 12. b (510)
5. b (496) 13. e (512)
6. c (498) 14. d (513)
7. d (500) 15. b (514)
8. d (501)

179

Just for Fun: Some Additional Readings

Hennig, M., and Jarolinn, A. Women executives in the old-boy network. _Psychology Today_, January, 1977. A female corporate star must learn the informal rules of business behavior that males take for granted.

Buckout, R., and Ellision, K.W. The line up: A critical look. _Psychology Today_, June, 1977. An eyewitness is often a terrified victim. Can this person's confusion, or a police officer's prodding, send the wrong person to jail?

Bower, B. Consequences of captivity. _Science News_, March 21, 1981. The psychological changes undergone by hostages and POWs are examined.

Scarf, M. Images that heal: A doubtful idea whose time has come. _Psychology Today_, September, 1980. This article takes a critical look at the theory of O. Carl Simonton, a doctor who is convinced that despair and other "negative emotions" cause cancer and that victims can cure themselves with a special form of positive thinking.

CHAPTER 14

INDIVIDUAL DIFFERENCES IN BEHAVIOR: PERSONALITY

AND SOCIAL PSYCHOLOGY

Objectives:

1. Discuss the alternate approach to predicting human behavior, individual differences in reactions to the same social situation.

2. Trace the history of utilizing personality characteristics or traits in predicting behavior by 1) discussing early claims that "traits ruled all" (including tests of traits), 2) the later bias that traits are poor predictors of behavior and 3) the recent suggestion that, when measured properly, traits might predict behavior well after all.

3. What basic question confronts social psychologists with regard to traits? Discuss the following qualifications of traits: narrowness, each person is consistent on some traits and not on others and the power of situational forces that act on a behavior of interest.

4. Where do trait labels come from? Name the event that generated interest in what has become known as the "authoritarian personality." Describe the methods used to develop the measure of authoritarianism with emphasis on "item analysis" and define the term.

5. Give examples of items from the F scale, define "reliability" and "validity" and tell how these attributes were established for the F scale, with special attention to "construct validity." Also consider the relative merits of global traits like "friendliness" compared to subtraits that are more specific.

6. Give an example of a "correlation" and describe the response-response type of research as well as the stimulus-response type. Identify each type with correlational or experimental research. Also describe "integrated" research and tell how a stimulus variable like "propinquity" is moderated by a personality variable like "need for affiliation."

7. What is the alternative approach to waiting until drunk drivers kill and then throwing them into jail? Describe the personality groups identified by personality test responses in the work by Donovan and Marlatt (1982). What was the nature of the items on the personality test and how were the risk levels of the groups established?

8. Define "loneliness" and describe the aspects of loneliness that have been measured and investigated. Describe Russell et al.'s (1980) loneliness scale, how it was constructed and how it was validated.

9. Discuss the experiences of loneliness that we all share and shortcomings that likely determine chronic loneliness. Indicate the difference between being alone and being lonely. Describe the typical lonely person.

10. Describe the behaviors that are usual for lonely people, with special emphasis on the cynical outlook of such people.

11. Describe the procedures and results of the study by Brodt and Zimbardo (1981) which was addressed to changing a major component of loneliness, shyness. Describe how faulty beliefs about self and environment are corrected in "cognitive therapy" (see Table 14.4). Consider how "social skills training" and self-help can lead to an elimination of loneliness.

12. Describe the history of the Type A-Type B personalities, with emphasis on Friedman's original conception. Discuss the characteristics of type As and Bs, the Jenkins Activity Survey and childhood experiences of Type As, including birth order. Also indicate the early environmental experiences of developing Type As and the comparison of female professionals and home-makers on Type A characteristics.

13. Contrast Type A and Type B achievement related behavior and consider the "proofreading" study by Fazio et al. (1981). Also list the negative aspects of being a Type A, including inclination to coronary and cardiovascular problems.

14. Compare the interpersonal behaviors of Type As and Type Bs, with special emphasis on the role of masculinity. Also indicate how Type As fare at marriage.

15. Describe the recommendations to Type As for change that will lower the probability of heart attack (see Table 14.6). Discuss the media and face-to-face approaches to correcting negative aspects of Type A behavior, with emphasis on avoiding anger and time pressure. Note cautions with regard to the success and the appropriateness of changing Type A behavior.

16. Define "sniveling," "internal locus of control," and "external locus of control." Discuss Rotter's concepts of "expectancy," "value," and controlability of reinforcements as well as give examples of items from his I-E scale.

17. Describe the childhood experiences of internals and externals. Discuss the social and competitive behaviors of the two types. Who is most maladjusted, internals or externals? Discuss locus of control and achievement with emphasis on minority status. Consider the study by Earn (1982) involving the interaction between locus of control and amount of pay.

18. Discuss natural and contrived methods of changing locus of control. What are the advantages of change in the direction of internality?

Who Done It?

Credit each of the concepts, theories, critical studies or important ideas listed below to the person or persons associated with each (e.g., item: Id-Ego-Superego; associated person: Freud). Answers are on the next page.

1. classified drivers who drink as to personality and risk of accident

2. used a "proofreading" task to study achievement behavior of Type As and Type Bs

3. inventor of the "internal-external" personality classification

4. developed the Activity Survey that measures Type A and Type B orientation

5. investigated the interaction between locus of control and pay

6. studied changing shyness

7. developed the UCLA Loneliness scale

Define

Each of the critical concepts listed below have been defined in your textbook. For each provide the definition. Answers are on the next page.

1. reliability

2. validity

3. construct validity

4. correlational research

5. experimental research

6. integrated research

7. loneliness

8. sniveling

Who Done It Answers

1. Donovan and Marlett (538)
2. Fazio and colleagues (552)
3. Rotter (531)
4. Jenkins (550

5. Earn (550)
6. Brodt and Zimbardo (544)
7. Russell and colleagues (540)

Definitions

1. the consistency with which any instrument measures a variable (535)

2. whether the test measures what it is supposed to measure (535)

3. the series of relationships that are established between test scores and other theoretically relevant responses (535)

4. the study of RESPONSE-RESPONSE RELATIONSHIPS because test responses are correlated with some other behavioral response (537)

5. the study of STIMULUS-RESPONSE RELATIONSHIPS in which a stimulus variable is manipulated, and its affect on a response variable is determined (537)

6. basing predictions of behavior on both traits and of stimulus variables (537)

7. the subjective experience of lacking close interpersonal relationships (540)

8. influencing fate (555)

Matching

This exercise appears on the next page. Match each concept on the left with an identifying phrase, word, or sentence on the right. Answers are at the bottom of the page. Cover them with a piece of paper.

A. authoritarianism
B. expectancy
C. item analysis
D. value
E. critical question about
   traits
F. "traits rule all"
G. Type A personality

_E_ 1. what traits are important in
       which situations
_G_ 2. inclined to coronary problems
_F_ 3. earliest claim regarding
       individual differences on
       characteristics
_A_ 4. F-Scale
_C_ 5. correlating items on a test
       with one another
_B_ 6. prediction that a behavior
       will lead to reinforcement
_D_ 7. worth of a reinforcement

Is Something Wrong Here?

For each statement below indicate what is wrong about the statement, if anything. If there is something wrong, answer "yes" and
indicate what's wrong. If nothing is wrong, answer "no, this one is
correct." At the end of this exercise you will find the answers.

1. Cognitive therapy involves changing beliefs about self and the
   reactions of others to self.

2. "Internal locus of control" refers to control of reinforcement
   residing in mysterious internal forces that the individual cannot manipulate.

3. Type As tend to be born second or later among the children in
   their families.

4. Lonely people tend to have deficits in social skills and there-
   fore can benefit from "social skill training."

5. In the construction of the UCLA LONELINESS SCALE, Russell and
   colleagues first selected items, then administered them to
   various groups, finding which were related to one another.

6. Media advertisements have proven to be superior to face-to-face
   approaches to changing Type A behavior.

7. Propinquity determines friendship relationships, regardless of
   "need for affiliation."

Matching Answers

1. E (532)   4. A (535)
2. G (553)   5. C (535)
3. F (531)   6. B (555)
              7. D (555)

185

Is Something Wrong Here Answers

1. No; this one is correct. (544)

2. Yes. Tusk, tusk (assuming you thought this one was correct)-- internal locus of control refers to the belief one has control over reinforcements. (555)

3. Yes; Type As tend to be first born. (551)

4. No; this one is correct. (544)

5. No; this one is correct. (540)

6. Yes; Certainly not; it's apparently the other way around. (548)

7. Yes; Not if the text author's hypothesis is correct. Propinquity would determine friendship relationships only for those who are high in need for affiliation. (540)

True-False

Indicate whether each of the following statements is true or false. Correct answers are at the end of this exercise.

1. There is no alternative to jailing drunk drivers.

2. In their original work, Friedman and Roseman (1959) described Type A persons as hard working, aggressive and always in a hurry.

3. Perhaps surprisingly, female homemakers surpass female professionals in Type A characteristics.

4. Individual differences in reaction to the same social situation is a legitimate alternative to the usual social psychological approach to understanding human behavior.

5. Mischel's argument that behavior is not transsituationally consistent increased the importance psychologists attached to traits.

6. As children, Type A persons tend to be rejected by parents who generally are indifferent to them.

7. Lonely persons tend to have a cynical outlook on life.

True-False Answers

1. Wrong; study of the personality traits of drivers who drink can lead to their identification and possible change. (538)

2. True. (547)

3. False; it is the other way around. (551)

4. True. (531)

5. False; it did just the opposite, since traits are based on transsituational consistency. (532)

6. False; parents of Type A persons tend to set high standards for them and push them hard. (551)

7. True. (546)

Fill-in-the-Blanks

Complete the following statements by filling in the blanks with correct information. The answers are at the end of this exercise.

1. Women who suffer_____ show a rise in externality.

2. While the parents of internals tend to be_____,

    those of externals tend to be _____.

3. Minority people tend to score to the _____ end of

    the I-E scale, which may account for the low level of

    _____ motivation that some claim for them.

4. In general, people who score to the _____ end

    of the I-E scale tend to be better adjusted than those who

    score to the _____ end.

5. According to research, females who were high in Type _____

    behavior and low in _____ were depressed and socially

    anxious.

6. One danger in changing Type As is that you may eliminate some

    highly _____ behavior in the process.

7. Relative to Type B males, Type As reported less _____ with their wives, more time spent in _____ activities at home, and a lower _____ and _____ duration of marital sex.

8. Just about every person is likely to feel lonely after their family has _____ or during a prolonged _____.

9. Among qualifications of traits that seem necessary for adequate predictions to be based on them are making them _____, realizing that each person is _____ for some traits and not others and understanding that when situational forces are _____, traits are not likely to determine behavior.

10. Interest in the authoritarian personality was generated by _____.

11. Traits may be weak predictors of behavior if these are improperly _____.

Fill-in-the-Blank Answers
1. divorce (also wife abuse) (559)
2. affectionate (also protective, approving); rejecting (also hostile, critical) (556)
3. external; achievement (557)
4. internal; external (557)
5. A; masculinity (554)
6. successful (effective, useful or other equivalent) (549)
7. communication; work-related; frequency; briefer (554)
8. relocated; illness (541)
9. narrower; consistent; powerful (533)
10. World War II (or events related to the same, such as dictators coming to power) (534)
11. measured (532)

1. Personality psychology is a field that concentrates on
   a. the influence of external forces on people
   b. the influence of people on other people
   c. the influence of variable internal forces on people (e.g., hormone cycles in women)
   d. the influence of stable characteristics which determine different responses to the same situation on the part of different people

   d.

2. Early global measures of personality were designed to assess basic personality and thus to predict behavior in
   a. specific situations only
   b. a series of related situations
   c. response to quite a wide variety of situations
   d. any individual regardless of who that person might be, as all persons were assumed to behave the same

   c

3. After the initial faith in the utility of traits for the prediction of behavior, during the 50s and the 60s
   a. some began to doubt whether traits would predict behavior in specific situations
   b. some began to suggest that behavior is not consistent across different situations
   c. some began to argue that consistency of behavior is an illusion
   d. all of the above

   d

4. "Energetic" is a good example of a _____ trait.
   a. broad
   b. worthless
   c. narrow
   d. abstract

   a

5. Of the original list from which modern trait labels come
   a. all words have received extensive attention by researchers
   b. fewer than 16 have been given extensive attention by researchers
   c. 171 nonoverlapping terms have been identified
   d. about 5,000 have been intensively investigated

   c

6. Endorsement of which of the following items would lead to increasing the respondent's authoritarianism score?
   a. all men are created equal
   b. sex is dirty and should be restricted to having babies
   c. it is good to be tender
   d. both a and c

   b

7. "Response-Response" research is sometimes referred to as
   a. correlational
   b. experimental
   c. anecdotal
   d. abstract

   a

8. Which of the following signify one of the groups of drivers identified in Donovan and Marlatt's (1982) study of driving and drinking?
   a. aggressive while driving
   b. high in depression and resentment
   c. drives for tension reduction
   d. all of the above

9. Scores on the UCLA Loneliness Scale correlated with which of the following?
   a. number of attempts at suicide
   b. number of temper tantrums
   c. number of episodes of depression
   d. number of weekends spent by oneself

10. Among the typical behaviors of lonely people are
    a. ask a lot of questions
    b. continue talking about topics others bring up
    c. a tendency to be too optimistic
    d. resorting to wish-fulfillment fantasy

11. Cognitive therapy often involves
    a. assessing clients' patterns of friendship
    b. lecturing clients on the foolishness of their assumptions about others
    c. assuming that the client's problem is inability in starting a relationship
    d. all of the above

12. Type As tend to be
    a. sociable
    b. aggressive
    c. relaxed
    d. both a and c

13. In comparing female professionals with homemakers, it was found that the former compared to the latter as being
    a. higher in Type A characteristics
    b. lower in Type A characteristics
    c. higher or lower in Type A characteristics, depending on the type of profession considered
    d. less equal to men on Type A characteristics

14. In comparison to Type Bs, Type As' interpersonal behavior
    a. reflects a belief that they are able to predict what others will do
    b. involves a prediction that in competition, they will win more money
    c. tends to be masculine, regardless of their biological sex
    d. all of the above

15. In a large Stanford University face-to-face program
    a. participants practiced Type B behavior
    b. participants advised one another
    c. participants were taught to avoid situations that evoke characteristic behavior
    d. all of the above

16. "External locus of control" is
    a. trying to influence one's fate
    b. controlling one's internal states
    c. feeling that one is a helpless pawn of the fates
    d. the belief that there is a "controller" like a "soul"
       located somewhere in the body

17. As children, internals
    a. have parents who expect them to be independent
    b. are rejected
    c. are treated in a protective manner by parents
    d. both a and c

Multiple Choice Answers

Just for Fun: Some Additional Readings

Hitler's Diaries, Newsweek, First half of May, 1983. What was Hitler
    really like? Surprisingly, the fake diaries "discovered"
    recently accurately paint half the picture. As the "diaries"
    indicate, in terms of his private personality he was bland,
    empty and generally uninteresting. However, the authors of the
    forgeries left out the truly dark side of The Fuehrer's person-
    ality.

The Modern Prince, Psychology Today, beginning in 1983. Niccolo
    Machiavelli was an Italian statesman who believed in manipulating
    other people (there is even a psychological scale named after
    him). One would well be wary of such a personality. You can
    learn all about Machiavellian types, and have a few laughs while
    you're at it, by following the Modern Prince.

Haskell, M. Women in the Movies, Psychology Today, January, 1983,
    p. 18. A stereotype is a set of traits that individuals assign
    to an entire group of people. In a way the stereotype of the
    group is the "personality" of the group, according to the per-
    ceptions of outsiders. The stereotype of women is changing for
    the better and the metamorphosis is reflected in current movies.

Young feminists speaking for themselves, Ms., April 1983, p. 43.
    With the changes in society, the personalities of individual
    women are becoming more complex and more unique. On the cutting
    edge of that change are the young feminists. It would be a good
    idea for young men to read this article...and young women too.

Burka, J. and Yeun, L. Mind games procrastinators play. Psychology
    Today. Procrastination is not a matter of time management.
    It's rebellion, fear of doing poorly, or too well.

Treichel, J.A. Type A personality; the phsyical response. Science
    News, October 30, 1982. Want to know how being a Type A leads
    to heart attacks? The physiological link is covered in this
    article.

CHAPTER 15

SEXUALITY: INTIMATE INTERPERSONAL BEHAVIOR

Objectives

1. Compare different contemporary societies in terms of orienta-
    tion to sexual matters and compare today with "yesteryear."
    How have media displays of sexuality evolved?

2. Discuss the implications of the "sexual revolution." How has it
    influenced males and females and the sexual difference between
    them and which kinds of behaviors and attitudes have increased
    and which have decreased over the course of the revolution?

3. Discuss the negative effects of the revolution, paying atten-
    tion to the philosophical problems of evaluating those effects.
    What problems concerning expectation have arisen and how has
    the revolution influenced adolescent sexuality? Consider impli-
    cations with regard to the transmission of genital diseases.

4. Describe how human sexuality differs from that of animals. Pay
    special attention to the role of pheromones by contrasting the
    importance of these for humans and lower animals.

5. Look at the way we regard "attractiveness," with attention to
    differences in importance of attractiveness for the sexes.
    Discuss the changes in the characteristics that are considered
    to be attractive in women.

6. Discuss the paradox involved with changes in the roles played by
    males and females in the "mating game." How do males and
    females regard potential partners with varying degrees of
    sexual experience? Describe the fantasies of people with
    "unusual sexual orientations."

7. What is the current status of homosexuality according to psychiatrists? Discuss "homophobia" and variations in sexual
   preference. Consider biological and learning theories of homosexuality with emphasis on "frustration," "cultural" and
   "parental" forms of the latter. How has Storms supported his
   theory of homosexuality.

8. Discuss the potency of sexual fantasy, including how it might be
   used therapeutically and its influences on current and subsequent
   sexual behavior. What is the stuff out of which fantasies are
   made? Pay attention to sex differences in fantasy and when
   fantasies occur.

9. Describe the sources of sexual arousal, the sexual response
   cycle, and the instruments used for studying sexual arousal.
   How is it that people are able to become aroused by someone
   else's sexual activity? Discuss how interference with attention
   to erotica influences reactions to the same. How does fear and
   anxiety influence reactions to erotica?

10. Discuss the level of availability of sexual material in the
    media and people's reactions to the presence of such material.
    What are the influences of erotica on reactions to others and
    how does erotica influence motivation to behave sexually and
    to copy the sexual behavior of models? How does attending
    to erotica influence anxiety about sex and plans to engage in
    the same?

11. Describe the relationship between early exposure to erotica
    and commission of sex crimes. Discuss what happened to the
    sex-crime-rate when erotica became readily available in Denmark.
    What happens when males are exposed to sexually violent
    portrayals?

12. Describe the nature of most studies on how exposure to erotica
    influences behavior and attitudes. What do these typical studies
    show concerning the duration of effects due to exposure to
    erotica and the affective responses to repeated exposure to the
    same erotica?

13. Describe the procedures of the Zillman and Bryant (1983) study
    of long term exposure to erotica. Discuss the influences of
    such exposure on affective responses to various unusual forms of
    sexual behavior and attitudes toward women and sex crimes.
    Do results mean all erotica should be eliminated?

14. Define "erotophobial" and "erotophilia." Demonstrate measures
    of the concepts by reference to Abramson and Imai-Marques'
    (1982) study of Japanese Americans. Describe the various ways
    that measures of erotophobia can be used to predict sexual
    behavior.

15. How did Fisher (1980) investigate the affects of erotophobia on learning and what did he find? What are the implications of erotophobia for behavior related to health?

16. Is it inadequate knowledge or erotophobia that accounts for the shocking avoidance of contraception among sexually active young people? Give examples of misconceptions about sexuality and contraception and indicate what Gerrard et al. (1982) found when they studied "information only" and "cognitive restructuring."

Who Done It?

Credit each of the concepts, theories, critical studies or important ideas listed below to the person or persons associated with each (e.g., item: Id-Ego-Superego; associated person: Freud). The correct answers are on the next page.

1. first important comprehensive research on human sexuality
   Kinsey & Pomeroy

2. very recently produced evidence that smell may play a role in human sexuality *Bauer*

3. presented some subjects with 36 sex films
   Zillman & Bryant

4. studied three generations of Japanese Americans
   Abramson & Imai-Marquez

5. studied the influences of erotophobia on learning
   Fisher

6. showed how "cognitive restructuring" can eliminate misconceptions among sexually active females
   Gerrard et al.

Define

Each of the critical concepts listed below have been defined in your textbook. For each provide the definition. Answers are on the next page.

1. pornography *material designed primarily to bring about sexual thoughts and sexual excitement*

2. genital herpes *an as yet incurable viral infection of the genitalia which is transmitted by sexual contact.*

3. penile plethysmograph *an instrument used to measure the physiological effects of male sexual arousal*

4. pheromone *a hormone yielding a scent that is a sexual attractor*

5. photoplethysmograph *an instrument used to measure the physiological effects of female sexual arousal*

6. plateau *the phase of continued sexual stimulation defined by Masters and Johnson*

7. sexual revolution *changes toward greater sexual permissiveness and variety of sexual activities which has taken place over the past 20 years*

195

8. homophobia : *the fear that homosexuals might inflict their preferences on others.*
9. ertophilia : *extremely positive attitudes about sexual matters*

Who Done It Answers

1. Kinsey and Pomery (569)
2. Baron (577)
3. Zillmann and Bryant (597)
4. Abramson and Imai-Marques (595)
5. Fisher (600)
6. Gerrard et al. (601)

Definitions

1. has sometimes been defined as material that is designed primarily to bring about sexual thoughts and sexual excitement; i.e., to titilate, to appeal to prurient interest (588)

2. as yet incurable viral infection of the genitalia (573)

3. an instrument designed to provide a physiological measure of male sexual arousal (585)

4. hormone yielding a scent that is a sexual attractor (574)

5. an instrument designed to provide a physiological measure of female sexual arousal (585)

6. phase of "continued sexual stimulation" (585)

7. the increase in interest in sexual matters and in sexual activity that has occurred over the last couple of decades (566)

8. fear that homosexuals might inflict their preferences on others (580)

9. extremely positive attitude about sexual matters (595)

Matching

Match each concept on the left with an identifying phrase, word or sentence on the right. The answers are on the next page.

A. U.S. and Soviet Union
B. fear and anxiety
C. sex guilt
D. persons who have unusual tastes
E. early exposure to erotica
F. male sexual fantasy
G. heat-sensitive photographic plates
H. more potent than "porno" for generation of sexual excitement
I. theoretical model of change in sexual responses during intercourse

_D_ 1. fantasy about being spanked
_F_ 2. being raped by several persons
_G_ 3. foundation of the "thermograph" measure of sexual excitement
_A_ 4. different stages of the "sexual revolution"
_H_ 5. fantasy
_C_ 6. associated with little mention of sex organs during report of sexual fantasy
_I_ 7. Sexual Response Cycle
_B_ 8. increases sexual arousal
_E_ 9. decreases likelihood of sex crimes

Is Something Wrong Here?

For each statement below indicate what is incorrect about the statement if anything. If there _is_ something wrong, answer "yes" and indicate what's wrong. If nothing is wrong, answer "no; this one is correct." The answers are on the next page.

correct
1. Storms hypothesizes that conditioning underlies sexual attraction, including to the same sex.

wrong
2. The paradox concerning the roles males and females play in the "mating game" is that males state they want females to be ~~passive~~, but then react badly when they get their wish. *assertive*

wrong assertive
3. Currently, psychiatrists still regard homosexuals as _not_ having emotional problems.

correct
4. When Zillmann and Bryant (1983) had some of their male subjects view 36 sexually explicit films, they became more calloused toward women.

wrong
5. Over time, there has been an increase in the frequency of most sexual behaviors, ~~including~~ visits to prostitutes by males. *except*

correct
6. People become sexually aroused by exposure to someone else's sexual activities by imagining themselves as a participant in the scene to which they are exposed.

wrong
7. Sex offenders tend to have experienced erotica *later* ~~earlier~~ than non-sex-offenders.

197

wrong
8. Measures of "erotophobia" are useful, ~~but cannot~~ *and can* be used to accurately predict actual sexual behavior.

correct
9. A viable alternative to elimination of all erotica would be to carefully examine the content of the same.

Matching Answers

1.	D	(582)	5.	H	(583)	9.	E	(593)
2.	F	(584)	6.	C	(598)			
3.	G	(585)	7.	I	(585)			
4.	A	(567)	8.	B	(587)			

Is Something Wrong Here? Answers

1. No; this one is correct. (581)

2. Yes; males state they want females to be assertive and active, but if they are, relationships don't tend to last. (579)

3. Yes; currently homosexuals are seen as not necessarily emotionally disturbed. (580)

4. No; this one is correct. (597)

5. Yes and no; all behaviors have increased, except visits to prostitues by males. (571)

6. No; this one is correct. (586)

7. A lot of people believe this statement, but it is not true; substitute "later" for "earlier." (592)

8. Yes; such measures may be used to predict sexual activity level and other behaviors. (599)

9. No; this one is correct. (597)

True-False

Indicate whether each of the following statements is true or false. Correct answers are at the end of this exercise.

T 1. Sexual material, at least of the "soft porno" variety, is more prevalent in the media (e.g., TV) than ever before.

F 2. Erotophobic women are over-concerned about their health, as manifested in highly frequent breast examinations.

198

3. Arousal due to exposure to erotica in the typical study tends to be of long duration.

4. Only since the last century have depictions of sex been available in any form.

5. The only remaining difference between popular sexual magazines such as <u>Playboy</u> and the hardcore porno found only in special shops is that erection, penetration, and ejaculation occur only in porno publications.

6. Interference with attention to erotica tends to lower arousal to the same.

7. Few people have had trouble meeting the modern expectation that one should be highly sexually active.

8. The number of teenage pregnancies per year in the U.S. has risen to 100,000.

9. According to the text, where cencorship of erotica has been totally lifted, as in Denmark, there has been a decline in sex crimes.

10. Teaching people to adequately engage in sexual fantasy may overcome many sexual problems.

<u>True-False Answers</u>

1. True (588)

2. False; they are less likely to use the breast exam. (600)

3. False; it tends to be of short duration (596)

4. False; displays having sexual meaning have always been present in art. (568)

5. True (568)

6. True (586)

7. False; some have had great difficulty meeting the new standard. (572)

8. False; the figure is 1,000,000. (572)

9. True (593)

10. True (583)

Fill in the Blanks

Complete the following statements by filling in the blanks with correct information. The answers are at the end of this exercise.

1. It is more important for a _female_ to be attractive than for a _male_ (reference is to the sexes).

2. _Large_ breasts were once considered attractive, but not today.

3. In terms of time and place, sexual fantasies may occur _at any time, any place night or day_.

4. Generally speaking, males and females found _highly_ sexually experienced strangers to be undesirable.

5. Compared to _erotophobic_ persons, _erotophilic_ persons attend church infrequently and are not embarrassed to talk about sex.

6. The source of fantasies may be _past memories_, themes borrowed from the _the media_ and/or _original_ creations.

7. Sex guilt is associated with _low_ contraceptive use.

8. In one study of interference with arousal during exposure to erotica, for females complex tasks interfered with arousal due to _auditory & visual_ erotica, and for males, the complex task interfered with arousal due to _auditory_ erotica.

Fill-in-the-Blanks Answers

1. female; male (578)
2. Large (579)
3. at any time, day or night (584)

4. highly (582)
5. erotophobic, erotophilic (595)
6. memories of past experiences; media; original (583)
7. low (601)
8. auditory and visual; auditory (586)

b 1. The only remaining difference between popular sexual magazines such as <u>Playboy</u> and the hardcore porno found only in special shops is
   a. males and females displayed together in the nude occurs only in porno publications
   b. erection, penetration, and ejaculation occur only in porno publications
   c. display of the genitals occurs only in porno publications
   d. all of the above

d 2. Concerning the goodness or badness of contemporary sexual practices, research
   a. has already told us whether it is good or bad
   b. will eventually tell us whether it is good or bad
   c. may eventually tell us whether it is good or bad
   d. can never tell us whether it is good or bad

d 3. Herpes can be contracted
   a. upon any contact with an infected person
   b. upon any sexual contact with an infected person
   c. upon any occasion of sexual intercourse with an infected person
   d. upon any occasion of sexual intercourse with an infected person for whom blisters are present

a 4. When Baron (1980) varied the type of clothes and the presence of perfume worn by a female collaborator, he found that male subjects were most attracted to the collaborator when she
   a. dressed informally (jeans and sweatshirt) and wore perfume
   b. dressed formally (blouse, skirt and hose) and wore no perfume
   c. dressed informally and wore no perfume
   d. dressed formally and wore perfume

d 5. Currently, when females are outgoing and take some initiative in relations with males
   a. males are likely to say their behavior is a positive development
   b. a resulting dating relationship is not likely to last
   c. males may interpret their behavior as seductive, flirtatious, and even promiscuous
   d. all of the above

d 6. Homophobia is
   a. rare
   b. true of most people
   c. nonexistent currently
   d. widespread

b 7. Among the example sex fantasies provided by female college students was
   a. being attacked by several men
   b. having intercourse with two males
   c. typing a male up and spanking him
   d. having intercourse astride a horse

8. Which of the following supports Storm's conditioning theory of homosexuality?
   a. people who mature late as opposed to early are more likely to be homosexual
   b. people who have parents that reinforce homosexuality tend to become homosexuals
   c. people who mature early as opposed to late are more likely to be homosexual
   d. people who are reared in a dviant subculture tend to become homosexual

9. When subjects were prevented from fantasizing while listening to an account of sexual behavior
   a. they became all the more aroused (relative to fantasizing subjects)
   b. sexual arousal did not occur
   c. sexual arousal was the same as it was for fantasizing subjects
   d. the individual differences in arousal were too great to allow for drawing any conclusions

10. When Barlow et al. (1982) had males anticipate electric shock while viewing explict erotica, they found
    a. enhancement of sexual arousal
    b. inhibition of sexual arousal
    c. no influence on sexual arousal
    d. a smaller sexual arousal response than was shown by females under the same conditions

11. Heiby and Becker (1980) found that female subjects engaged in masturbation_____ frequency after viewing a model practice the behavior, compared to before viewing.
    a. at a lower   c. at a higher
    b. at a much lower   d. at the same

12. Most effects due to exposure to erotica
    a. involve mere imagination   c. involve only simple nudity
    b. last for several days   d. last for an hour or less

13. An alternative to elimination of all erotica due to its negative effects would be
    a. examine the content of erotica more closely
    b. make erotica off-limits to anyone under 30
    c. make erotica unavailable, except in government-controlled outlets
    d. limit erotica to single-sex portrayals only (male and female interaction eliminated)

14. Abramson and Imai-Marques (1982) compared sexual attitudes of
    a. today's Japanese and Japanese-Americans
    b. first-, second-, and third- generation Japanese-Americans
    c. Americans of pure Japanese descent with those of mixed Japanese-American ancestors
    d. Americans with Japanese-Americans

15. Fisher (1980) studied the influences of erotophobia on academic performance. His subjects
    a. were enrolled in a course in human sexuality
    b. were enrolled in an introductory psychology course
    c. were tested over psychological material
    d. were given a test of general abilities

16. Among teenagers, widely held beliefs about contraception include which of the following?
    a. the use of contraception is a sin
    b. contraception use increases the likelihood of pregnancy
    c. the use of contraception is unromantic
    d. both a and c

Multiple Choice Answers

1.	b	(568)	9. b	(586)
2.	d	(572)	10. a	(587)
3.	d	(573)	11. c	(591)
4.	a	(577)	12. d	(596)
5.	d	(579)	13. a	(597)
6.	d	(580)	14. b	(595)
7.	b	(584)	15. a	(600)
8.	c	(581)	16. c	(601)

Just for Fun: Some Additional Readings

Goleman, Daniel, and Bush, S. The liberation of sexual fantasies.
    Psychology Today, October, 1977. Let your mind go! Cultivate
    your wildest fantasies! Or should you?

Cramer, R. The new double standard. Psychology Today, June, 1983.
    "Double standard" you say? Now you could speak of the "double-
    double standard." Today's women join men in expecting stricter
    morality of the opposite sex than of their own sex.

Adams, V. Male strippers' lusty female fans. Psychology Today,
    April, 1983. Guess who's patronizing the strip joints these
    days? We won't tell, but she's having a wild, old time.

Zibergeld, B. Pursuit of the Grafenberg spot. Psychology Today, Oct.
    1982. Breakthrough! A book by Alice Ladas, Beverly Whipple and
    John Perry claims the discovery of a hyper-sensitive "G" spot in
    the vagina. Unfortunately, the facts are thin.